HIDDEN BRILLIANCE

A **HIGH-ACHIEVING INTROVERT'S** GUIDE TO SELF-DISCOVERY,
LEADERSHIP AND **PLAYING BIG** **KATIE RASOUL**

Publishing Services provided by Paper Raven Books
Printed in the United States of America
First Printing, 2018

Paperback ISBN= 978-0-9998069-0-6
Hardback ISBN= 978-0-9998069-1-3

To my husband Jason, who makes everything more fun and more possible.

To Nolan, who was the turning point for realizing just how grand life could be.

To baby, who reminds me daily to honor the present.

TABLE OF CONTENTS

PART I: THE STORY

"Speak the truth, even if your voice shakes."
– *Unknown*

INTRODUCTION

It took me 34 years to realize that some of the rules I lived my life by were not inherent to everyone. You know when you have only ever known one way, and so it didn't ever even occur to you that there might be others? That was what I realized this year.

It is a bit jarring, in fact, regardless of what the old or new truth is, to all of a sudden become aware of an entirely new path. You can't help but ask yourself, "Was that always here? Why didn't I notice it before?" It is also totally normal to ask yourself, "What is true? Is this old truth that I've held for decades right, or has my whole life been a lie?"

Okay, so it doesn't have to be so binary, but hell, sometimes it feels like it is.

Hidden brilliance is not about intellect or hard work that can't be seen. It is about a life beyond valuing achievement. It is the idea that once you move beyond your own limiting beliefs, there is a whole other level of awesome life that is available to you once you simply unlock the door and are brave enough to cross the threshold.

In this book, I will share with you my own personal journey through climbing the ladder, exiting corporate America, and staring face-to-face with the personal turning point to have a whole new understanding of achievement in life. The purpose of this book is for you to experience a glimpse into the unknown through the thoughts and feelings of a high-achieving introvert waking up in the world. My hope is that you will see yourself in this story and use the journey as a catalyst for your own awakening towards an incredible, brilliant life.

The second half of the book will take you through some of the same activities that were critical in my voyage to clarity and are here to serve you as well. See yourself in the story, and recreate the personal growth for yourself.

Go forward now. Here is the real me, and I can't wait to meet the real you.

CHAPTER 1: THE WEIGHT

"Moderation is a fatal thing. Nothing succeeds like excess." – Oscar Wilde

In sports, it is common practice to add extra resistance when you train so that when it comes time for the real competition, your body feels lighter and easier to move than when you trained, preparing you to give your best performance when it matters most. In the same way that weightlifters add extra pounds to their barbells and race car drivers add extra drag to their cars, I have been carrying a weight for decades, training for this moment. All of my life, I have been preparing for something really big.

It wasn't until the weight became unbearable that I even realized it was there. The weight I felt was a heavy load made of a sense of responsibility, a need for achievement, and a tendency to go "all in" on life. In a matter of a handful of moments, at the age of 34, I realized that I had been carrying around something very heavy with me practically my entire life.

I have always been intrinsically motivated, constantly driven to achieve big things by plans of my own creation. I chose my path based on how I would view it for myself or how it made me feel. At first glance, this approach to life feels very self-aware or forward thinking. I assure you, though, that it was not, because it was clouded by rules and filters that I had imposed on myself and that simply didn't serve me. Perhaps this approach did serve me at one time. I can't begin to fathom what my life would be like had I not been the conscientious, Type A rule follower I was when I was growing up. Would life have turned out the same? Or would countless tiny decisions of lesser quality have added up to me being an unmotivated degenerate that never amounted to much? If this type of drive ever did serve me well, at some point, it stopped.

After years working for large companies and corporate environments, I started my own company. I loved the work that I was doing in talent development and organizational culture, and I wanted to add in a professional coaching model to my work. I now serve as a professional leadership coach, and strategic advisor for leadership development, company culture, and the employee experience. I have the opportunity to help high-potential leaders realize even bigger and more fulfilling lives through coaching, and it is my purpose in this world.

In the first year of business, this personal drive of mine, which has always gotten me where I needed to go, finally came to a tipping point. I was now my own boss, the only person laying out the goals and expectations, and the weight started to feel unbearable.

It was the same weight that I had always felt and managed to tolerate or ignore, but now it was getting heavier. I was feeling as if my whole body was being compressed, and I was fighting to keep my space. One day, like a lightning bolt, it struck me. I felt compelled to put what I was feeling into words. Then this sentence came to me:

I am being crushed by the rising expectations for greatness because I don't have anyone holding me back anymore.

There it was, written on a sticky note. After it came out of my pen, I just stared at it for a while. Well, shit. What did that mean, exactly? How did I even get to this point? And how do I move forward from here?

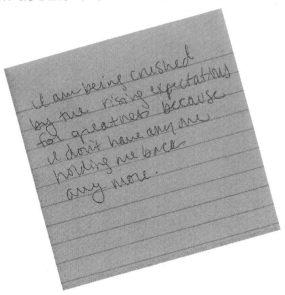

I was being crushed by the rising expectations for greatness. This phrase has double meaning for me. My own expectations of myself for greatness were rising because no one was there to tell me when I had done "good enough" so that I knew when to stop. At the same time, I had always needed and waited for other people's approval of "good enough," not just so I knew when to stop, but also because it let me off the hook for doing anything truly scary and great. I think the idea of doing something truly huge scared the shit out of me. So, now, I was being crushed by the fact that I was the only thing holding me back from being great. I no longer got to silently blame anyone else, or the system, for not allowing me to reach true greatness. The blame could only fall on me now.

Let me be clear: when I say "good enough," I really mean absolute excellence. This is the classic, skewed scale that many high-achievers use for themselves. I don't have to win, be first, be the best, or have the sole recognition. I have never been competitive or really cared about winning. What I care a ridiculous amount about is being truly excellent in everything that I do. So, when something is "good enough" for someone else, it means that it was the best meeting anyone has planned to date, or the most thorough, creative, and strategic plan that has ever been brought before the boss.

And this is where the weight gets heavier. As stakes got higher, roles at work got bigger, the importance of the outcomes and the pressure I put on myself got heavier and heavier. As an adult, because I couldn't remember a time without the weight, I didn't even notice it was there. I thought it was perfectly normal to over-prepare for every meeting or presentation, to feel stressed to strive for excellence in everything that I tried, and to be unable to honestly answer the questions "How are you?" or "Are you okay?" I either lied and said I was great, or I burst into tears without explanation. That was WAY too complex of a question for me to actually answer honestly.

When you take this weight and need for success and put it into life experiences that you simply can't control, things get stressful. Pregnancy, and subsequently parenting, were two of those situations for me. Both of these scenarios have been a wonderful experiment to teach me to chill the hell out, and that sometimes "done is better than perfect." Even though OF COURSE you know the best way to load the dishwasher, when you are ten weeks pregnant and just trying to survive the day without puking or falling asleep in a meeting, you have to come to terms with the fact that your amazing husband can load the dishwasher however he wants if it means you don't have to do it. As a parent, I had to realize I was much less annoyed playing with my toddler when I let go of how I thought you were "supposed" to play with a certain game, and just let him teach me.

I had carried this weight, this need for excellence and success, since I was old enough to care about anything. There is a principle I learned in coaching that says "How you do anything is how you do everything." The first time I heard that, it did not resonate with me. And, as I learned about the weight that I carry, that my need to do literally everything with excellence and to the best of my ability, it suddenly clicked. I do nearly everything in the world with the same drive for excellence. I find this to be different (albeit similar) to perfectionism, because I can't even define perfect. Excellence creates this upward opportunity to always get better, where perfectionism to me denotes more of an exact, perfect way.

The journey to free myself from this weight has taken me down many winding paths. Many of the treks I took are summarized in the exercises in Part 2. But before that, I had to learn more about myself. It turns out I had a lot to learn.

CHAPTER 2: THE HIGH-ACHIEVING INTROVERT

"Achievement is not about what you've done, but
what you've gained from your experience."
– Lynn Hill

Do all high-achieving introverts fight this internal battle with the heavy weight they place on themselves? Perhaps not all, but inevitably there is someone out there realizing for the first time that the weight they feel, possibly also self-induced, is there and it is heavy. For many of us introverts, there is a rich inner monologue that constantly strategizes and incessantly scans the environment to observe and take in information. When we pair that with intrinsic motivation, it can be a powerful base for intentional action.

Most people do not think of high-achievers as introverts or stereotypical introverts as high-achievers. We have a misunderstanding of what it is like to be a high-achiever or to be an introvert. I write this book with the understanding that high-achievers are self-motivated individuals with a certain mindset that drives their thoughts, feelings, and behaviors to certain outcomes of achievement. When the outside world sees "high-achiever," it is usually attached to someone who has earned a lot of awards or has accomplished a lot at a faster rate than others. Outwardly, we appear to be the people who are good at everything we do, and everything we touch seems to turn to gold. When I set my daily Google Alert update on the phrase "high-achiever," most of the articles featured young people who accomplished a lot very early in life, like 4.0 GPAs, perfect SAT scores, and athletic superiority. Only a handful of articles addressed the self-inflicted pressure high-achievers feel or the weight they feel thinking they are never doing enough. If they did, they appeared in the form of grim stories about high-achieving high school students who simply couldn't handle the pressure and turned to suicide.

High-achiever has been a buzzword for a while and seems fairly self-explanatory. Introvert, on the other hand, is more evasive, and the world seems to be in the beginning phases of truly comprehending what it means to be an introvert. Thanks to the work of Susan Cain's book, *Quiet*, online communities like *Quiet Revolution*, and Jenn Granneman's *Introvert, Dear*, the world has a better understanding of what introversion really is. Those of us who are introverts finally are starting to feel understood.

People tend to mistakenly categorize introverts as just being shy loners who don't like to talk to people. While that can be true, that is often not the case. I won't repeat the great work of Susan Cain and Jenn Granneman here, but the basics of introversion boil down to *how people respond to stimulation and how we receive or expend energy.* For our purposes here, we will think more about introverts and extroverts by how they gain or give energy. Extroverts tend to gain energy by being around other people and might dislike too much time in solitude. Conversely, introverts tend to gain energy by having quiet time alone and might feel drained after a lot of group time or a big party.

In businesses or other organizations, there is often a premium placed on leaders who show courage, share ideas in meetings, and perhaps showcase great work. And oftentimes those leaders are successful. However, many introverted leaders display a quiet strength that can be overlooked when the loudest voices are the ones most heard. Introverts are often misunderstood, especially high-achieving introverts who are usually successful without even realizing their full potential.

High-achievers who don't identify as introverts may find that they are more extrinsically motivated than their introverted counterparts. Extroverted high-achievers might thrive on competition and find it easy to speak up in meetings, use their voices, and articulate their big ideas to others. They may process ideas by talking out loud and working in groups, and may feel energized by big visions. High-achieving introverts still have big visions and great ideas but are more inclined to process them internally and tend to speak up only when there is something important to say. We may even feel overwhelmed by our own big ideas, because we are capable of receiving so much information through deep observation that it feels like drinking out of a fire hose.

Often when I read articles or books about introverts, particularly in the "career" chapters, I find myself saying "YES!" to the introversion tendencies but then feel a disconnect when suggestions about how to apply my new understanding as an introvert to daily life falls flat. On any given day, you can read articles about "handling collaboration at work," "surviving a job interview," or the misery of "open concept offices." The topics are never aiming high enough to reflect my own big dreams at work. I keep searching for literature that acknowledges my unique tendencies as an introvert and address high-achieving topics like, "leading the C-suite," or "tips for introvert leaders preparing for keynote speaking." They don't really exist.

If you have ever taken the Myers-Briggs Type Indicator (MBTI) personality assessment, you may have found a personality classification that suits you. I am considered an INFJ (Introversion | Intuition | Feeling | Judging) which is the rarest of all the classifications at only about 1.5% of all MBTI participants. I would vouch that we are a complex bunch: organized, decisive, committed, creative, and empathetic. Sharing can sometimes be challenging for introverts, particularly in leadership roles. For some, small talk may be painful. For others, sharing personal details with people who aren't in your inner circle feels wrong.

As an introverted leader myself, I can share a glimpse into my thoughts, and perhaps this may be helpful in understanding the "why" behind some observable behaviors:

- **Talking (or not):** I am an observer, a listener, and a thinker. It serves me and my team well in many ways. I prefer to talk when I have something impactful to share but don't prefer to speak as a way of processing my thoughts.

- **Quality over quantity:** In relationships, I prefer to have a few close people in my inner circle, rather than 30 best friends. The idea of sales "funnels," or finding more potential buyers to put in your business pipeline, annoys me because I prefer fewer, stronger relationships.

- **Leading:** I value one-on-one time with my team members and understand how to best tailor to each person's needs. I really listen and love complex problem-solving. Also, I see my team is my inner circle, so they get to know a lot more about me.

- **Thinking:** I am carefully calculated, hold high standards, and have meticulously thought about the potential outcomes of all options. It's like playing chess when most of the world is playing checkers.

- **Meetings:** I love an agenda and information sent in advance of the meeting so I can take time to well prepare my thoughts. Being asked on the fly feels like I do not have sufficient time to reflect on my answers.

Don't get me wrong, extroverts. We appreciate you, and we need you as both personalities are important. Many of you thrive under pressure and can talk through, brainstorm, and find solutions in the moment. You have gifts that work well in the world, and that we aim to emulate. I also implore leaders in organizations to listen for the less vocal members of their teams so as to not overlook the quiet strength and value that introverts may bring. For my fellow quiet leaders, find ways to share with others more about how you operate and what works for you. The more we can help others understand how we tick, the better we can work together.

The internal conflict between less and more presents another challenge for some introverts. The inner workings of a high-achieving introvert live at the intersection of the drive to achieve more and the need for solitude. The tension between ambition to be out conquering the world fighting and the need to be alone with our thoughts, means that high-achieving introverts are no strangers to big dreams that can feel overwhelming. Mahatma Gandhi once said, "In a gentle way, you can shake the world." We want to shake the world in a big way but without trumpets or fanfare or small talk, which means that we're not very good at including others in our feeling of accomplishment. The result: shame and fear of being "found out" as a fraud.

High-achievers often feel shame for not meeting their high expectations of themselves or for feeling like a fraud. We can feel the rising pressure to keep up with ourselves, assuming we can and should "do it on our own." We can be so focused on the future that we forget to enjoy the present. Combining drive and inner reflection can either serve as a superpower or a recipe for implosion.

The world today is filled with endless options and social media facades. As a result, we are conditioned to assume that "more is better" and that everyone is out living their best life, documented by glittery Facebook feeds. However, this "you can do anything, and more is better" narrative is not helping. Looking back, I know where I went wrong. When I heard "you can do anything," I replaced "anything" with "everything" and "can" with the almighty "should." Operating with the mindset of "I should do everything" inevitably leads to disappointment, shame, and a blow to the self-esteem. And I have found through my work and research on generational differences that this cultural shift does not only affect high-achieving introverts. Millennials report having the highest rates of depression and anxiety of any generation, and the next generation is following suit. We are in a unique moment to examine this idea now, and apply it to the rest of our lives and how we raise the next generation.

On a broader scale, we are part of a larger subculture of "outliers." Banded together by the mutual experience of feeling like "the other," we begin to question what is true for us, because what is true for us seems to go against the grain of what is true for everyone else. But just as we have perhaps often felt like outsiders, I encourage you to search for commonality and comfort in the fact that there is still a whole lot that makes us the same. While we all have our individual and unique take on life, we are all sharing one common human experience. Every emotion that we experience has been felt by someone else before, and we are not alone.

We all have inner critic voices telling us we aren't enough of something. They tell us to sit down or play small. For those addicted to achievement, this is the place where perfectionism breeds and where nothing is ever enough. I always thought that I needed this weight and that I was successful because of it, not in spite of it. But what would it be like to be a high-achiever without the weight? It would feel easy, free, present, and without fear of what might happen. But could I be successful without it? I had lived my whole life thinking that was the only path to success, when in reality, perhaps it was the one thing holding me back from my true greatness.

But it's probably best to start at the beginning.

CHAPTER 3: GROWING UP

"Time does not change us. It just unfolds us."
– Max Frisch

I was born in 1983, unknowingly plunked into what we now know to be a pretty bitchin' decade. Here are some notable features about 1983: Ronald Reagan was President, the Apple Lisa personal computer was released, the final episode of MASH aired, Michael Jackson showed us the Moonwalk, the cold war was ongoing, and *Return of the Jedi* was the highest grossing film of the year.

And this is me – making my big entrance into the world! Here is a picture of me, my sister, and my mom from that year. Please note that my sister just opened up an E.T. doll, and my mom is holding me on an orange velour chair. (I will also mention that those chairs spruced up the living room of my college apartment for several years.) Apparently, I was a good eater judging by my voluptuous baby rolls and that hungry look in my eyes warning my older sister that I may eat her at any moment.

I grew up in the suburbs (almost the country) in a small city in Wisconsin. My mom was a special education teacher turned school psychologist, and my dad worked as a civil engineer. It was a decidedly middle-class upbringing where we didn't eat very fancy food, but we also weren't lacking anything in our lives. I was given every opportunity to succeed (both by my parents and systemic privilege) and I made the most of those prospects. I competed on the swim team, dabbled in local theater, danced a lot, and had a nice group of friends. It all sounds very plain vanilla, and it was pretty low on the scale of strife and struggle. This upbringing provided me with an incredibly solid foundation for feeling comfortable in my own skin and instilled confidence that I was doing good things.

Right around my birthday in the fourth grade, my parents told my sister and me that they were divorcing. Adults and counselors kept reminding me that it "wasn't my fault" that my parents were getting a divorce. In my mind, it had never occurred to me that it would be my fault; that sounded silly to me. I remember crying at the time, because I felt sad for them and for our family, but never because I harbored emotional responsibility for the loss. After several years, the final result was two sets of very supportive parents, some additional step-siblings to boss me around, and the good fortune of twice the Christmas presents. That is about the extent of my personal trauma.

As a child, I remember teachers and coaches describing me with words like conscientious, committed, and responsible. Of my own accord, I filled all of my time with something: school, work, advanced placement classes. The best day for my parents in 1999 must have been the day I earned my driver's license so they could stop chauffeuring me around the city from activity to activity. I drove from theater practice to swim team and came home in time to eat a lukewarm plate of spaghetti my mom had saved for me at 8:30 p.m. I was tired enough at that point that I never bothered to heat up my food (and to this day I still tend to eat food at the same temperature). I would do homework on the couch until I fell asleep, would wake up in the middle of the night to keep working, and would somehow magically finish my homework before I hauled my ass to early morning swim practice or National Honors Society meetings again the next day.

Looking back, I have two vivid memories of feeling a certain weight on my shoulders in high school. They are the two moments in my youth when I can pinpoint instances when my carefully-curated exterior as a high-achiever cracked open and my true inner pressures and expectations showed up to the world around me. I am not bold enough to assume that I was so good at hiding it that no one could have possibly noticed, but no one had taken the opportunity to mirror those feelings back to me before these two incidents.

In my younger years around the age of nine, I was a very avid singer in my school choirs. In high school, I had the good fortune of being part of a very high quality and long-standing choral program with a choral director who was well-liked and slightly feared. It was a place where I found many of my friends in the other nerdy and interesting weirdos who saw the value and felt the love in making music. I can think back to my days in music and recognize that, although I wasn't the best singer, choir was one of the few places where I truly felt in my flow and operated in my highest possible form without care of what others were thinking or doing. At least, this was true when the music was being made.

Our teacher had some pretty strong student relationships, but not necessarily with me (I didn't often open up easily), which makes what happened next even more surprising. One day, we were at an off-site location for rehearsal leading up to a concert. I recall a specific moment when my choral teacher looked at me (as in,

REALLY looked at me and saw me) and asked me how I was doing. In that moment, it was the first time that I had ever really felt found out and truly seen. It was simultaneously overwhelming, scary, and relieving. I burst into tears as the weight I had always been carrying suddenly crushed me, as if somebody else seeing the weight suddenly made it real. No one had ever really looked closely enough to notice it before. I was surprised by the uncontrolled tears that were pouring down my face, but he looked as if he already knew (which, of course, he did). My teacher gave me a hug and let me cry for a minute before I pulled it back to my usual "I'm great!" self, and then I moved on by stuffing it all down into the box where I kept my feelings of being overwhelmed. It was a rare slip-up.

This is the first memory I have where my outsides ever so briefly matched my insides. It never manifested in the form of clinical depression or anxiety or something else big enough to warrant a diagnosis and action from others, but it was always there. It stayed and grew, taking up more and more space, getting heavier. It felt like the equivalent of slowly gaining weight, like putting on five pounds a year until you realize ten years down the road, that you gained 50 pounds before you noticed the "problem."

Along with music, dance played a key role as a place of passion and personal expression. I had taken dance classes since around the age of three, and the only time I tired of them was when I felt like I was no longer learning or growing enough, which I rectified by finding more challenging dance groups. One new dance studio that I moved to gave me the opportunity to take my first true contemporary style dance class. It was new, exciting, and slightly outside my comfort zone. The instructor for the class was sort of a hippie-ish alternative lady whom I loved. I always looked forward to her classes, and I think it was in part because, for the first time, someone paid pretty close attention to me.

One day at the start of class, the instructor handed each of us a blank piece of paper and a pencil. She asked each of us dancers to journal whatever was on our minds and gave us several minutes. We each found our little corner of space on the floor, sprawled out on our stomachs to write on the hardwood dance floor while she played instrumental music in the background. I recall having a particularly tough day that day, juggling lots of balls in the air. I took the opportunity to scrawl on about feeling overwhelmed and frustrated, as if there was some invisible monster forcing me to do all of this "stuff." After intensely writing for five minutes straight with a pencil on the hardwood, my hand started to cramp up. Writing my frustrations down had made me feel better, as if I had released some of the stress. At the end of our time, we handed our journaling in to the instructor and went on with class as usual, learning technique and dance combinations. She took them home to read.

The very next week in class, she shared with us what our dance presentation would be for the spring recital. It was a piece where each dancer would dance their own mini-solo to some recorded spoken words. She had selected a personal quality that best fit our thoughts from J. Ruth Gendler's *Book of Qualities*, where the author personifies different emotions and personality qualities, and vividly describes them as if they are people. After explaining the construct of the piece, she handed out pages to everyone that listed the personal quality she had selected for us based on what she knew about us already and our journaling from the previous week. As she handed pages to my peers, I heard the names of the qualities they would be representing: Patience, Stillness, Discipline. Then I looked at my piece of paper and read the word "Panic."

Here is an excerpt from the page on Panic:

> *Panic has thick curly hair and large frightened eyes. She has worked on too many projects meeting other people's deadlines. She wakes up in the middle of the night pulling her hair out. She is crying for help, but only when she is sure no one is around to hear her.*
>
> *Panic is sure no one can help her. She must sweat out these demons on her own. Although people care about her, she refuses to see them. She is ignoring the evidence of her own senses.*
>
> *– J. Ruth Gendler*

Other people personified calm or pleasant things. I had the anxious, thrashy part of the dance piece. I supposed having a variety of qualities made for a good work of art. At the time, I remember being a little annoyed for about a millisecond about my assignment but then just shrugged it off, thinking it made sense considering what I had written on my paper the week before. Truth be told, I really enjoyed dancing my part of the piece personifying Panic. It felt uniquely mine and accurate, and I appreciated the opportunity to dance out my frustration weekly.

It was not until more than fifteen years later that I looked back at that passage and had the willingness and openness to observe that not only was Panic the exact right match at that point in my life, but the words are also poignantly representative of my adult life. I realized I have always preferred angry, more expressive and honest dances. Ballet was never really my thing, because it was always a façade, like kabuki theater, rather than a true expression of emotion. I much preferred contemporary dance, or styles like krumping, which is a high-energy, high-expression variation of hip-hop dancing that was created on the streets of L.A. as a way to express anger and aggression in a positive way. Frustrated people, you should try it.

In college, the weight continued to grow. I was an Honors scholar and worked three jobs, not because I needed the money but because it was important to me to get the experience and apply myself as quickly as possible. Looking back, I can see that I was the poster child of collecting clubs, activities, projects, and responsibilities to make my own ridiculous collection of "stuff" that constantly kept me busy. I was often strategic in where I spent my time, like the Honors Club, the civic choir, and coveted application-only business school classes. Inevitably, I did things that looked good on the resume, even though I hated them. Finance Club? It was the worst, but I paid my dues and showed up, because I imagined it would be one of those key differentiators for my future employer. (Note: As someone who spent a lot of time in Human Resources looking at applications, I am certain nobody ever gave a shit about my participation in Finance Club, for the official record).

This makes it seem okay, right? When it is all good and important stuff that you spend your time on, you fail to see that perhaps you and all those around you would be better served by doing less and focusing more in-depth time on a few important areas. I did a lot, and with my personal insistence to be "all in" on everything that I did, it perpetuated the problems I had started early on of overcommitting my energy. This would continue to expand in my career.

At this point in college, I found myself starting to take everything personally, because I was so hard on myself. The standards that I had set for myself had grown from what were above average in high school, to truly suppressive by the end of college. Every move seemed to matter, as if it was the most important chess game of my life in order to secure the best career path. Apparently, I still hadn't learned the lesson from high school that nearly none of these things – grades, activities, classes – mattered as much as I thought they would in the end.

During college circa 2003, I happened to flip the channel to a reality television show called *Starting Over* where a group of women lived in a house and participated in coaching to overcome their own personal obstacles. I watched from my college apartment and the first time I heard there was such a profession as a "Life Coach," I was blown away. This was actually a thing? I studied Finance and French and was busy planning my future life as a jet-setting, suit-wearing international finance executive. But if I wasn't doing THAT (or independently wealthy), then I would most definitely be a life coach.

If I really wanted to play the "if I knew then" game, I would have maybe been a Psychology major instead, would have become a professional coach much earlier, and today Brené Brown and I would be best friends! My mom became a school psychologist after a mid-career change from teaching, so I should have known. But no, I was off chasing some definition of success and achievement that I hadn't fully thought through at that age, and that definitely wasn't true to my heart.

Instead, I graduated with a Finance degree, began working as a Human Resources Manager and continued to find new ways to expect more of myself and fear the day when the whole scheme of my success would unravel.

CHAPTER 4: THE "RIGHT" CAREER

"The question should be, is it worth trying to do, not can it be done." – Allard Lowenstein

Having spent most of my college time curating the right experience for the perfect career, I kept up the practice once I actually joined the workforce. I had already made one critical decision based on my gut when I decided to take a summer internship in retail management instead of a year-long internship in treasury finance, forgoing a career in finance for something more fun and aligned with my values and strengths as a leader. I had listened to my intuition, and it was the best decision I had ever made at that phase of my life. As a result, I felt very much in the "right place" – an environment where people understood me – and I felt a sense of belonging (an experience that eludes us high-achieving introverts sometimes as a side-effect of never quite feeling understood).

In my career, I continued the perpetual cycle of beating my expectations and then raising them, assuming that was the recipe for success. I worked long and hard hours, because like with everything, I was "all in." It only took a matter of months for me to start to burn out. A coworker and good friend stepped in to intervene and challenge the hours I was working. I needed that gut-check from the outside world to know when to stop, that I was doing enough, and that it was okay to go home. I only celebrated accomplishments when I impressed myself, and rarely did external recognition mean as much to me. The drive that had always been the cornerstone of my work kicked into high gear in a high-performing organization and went wild in a new adult world with fewer guardrails to define my time.

At work, I always felt torn between not concerning myself with what others thought and needing approval from someone important to ensure that I was on track. I learned that I am not very good at taking directions from other people, since I like to make the plans and execute them autonomously. Yet, when I couldn't tell if it was "good enough," I urgently needed someone's approval as a boundary test. The Imposter Syndrome ran deep within me, so seeking others' input was also a way to see if my cover was blown yet.

As I was selected for more leadership development programs, special groups for high-potentials, and promotions, the stakes got higher. I was excited and challenged by these experiences, yet fully aware that as my stock climbed, there was more at stake if it fell. If I hadn't been found out yet that I wasn't the leader everyone thought I was, then my own psyche had to up the ante to keep the ruse going. It felt like a bad Ponzi scheme, a total house of cards. I would start to feel the pressure, then have some success at work and go back to running my own ship until I had to check in at the scene of the crime to see if I'd been caught yet.

As my career grew, I found myself on the verge of cracking into tears more and more. I avoided the question of "How are you?" with anyone who was actually really listening for the answer, and tried to spit out an "I'm great! How are you?" deflection as quickly as possible to keep my inner monologue from spinning out of control and pushing tears out of my tear ducts without my control. I always chalked it up to being a sensitive person who cried easily at nearly everything, including sappy TV commercials. It seemed normal for me. It had always been this way as long as I could remember, since the first time I burst into tears in front of my choir director. Luckily for me with my inability to hold my shit together, I was the Human Resources person and one ever really asks how we are doing.

On paper, I had made all of the right moves. I had achieved everything that I set out to do, and I was supported and rewarded appropriately for it. And yet, somehow, it was just not as fulfilling as I knew it could be. I left the office most days feeling misunderstood and drained: misunderstood because I rarely found connection with others who shared my same mindset, work philosophies, and values, and drained because I worked so hard for what felt like small returns on an intrinsic investment. I had crafted the "right" career, so what was my problem? Why couldn't I feel more grateful for what I had? Why didn't I feel more deeply proud of the work I was doing? I felt as if I was doing good work but nothing that changed lives or that I could feel the effects of deep in my bones.

The work evolved, and I found myself further and further away from my center. I began to feel the pit in my stomach grow on Sundays in anticipation of the week ahead that was sure to be filled with big effort and no intrinsic rewards. I needed long stints out running by myself with just my thoughts and my headphones to counteract the stress. What I didn't realize until later is that these were all symptoms of feeling more and more out of alignment with who I was and the work that I was meant to be doing. It began to affect my health, my relationships, and my previously sunny disposition.

The problem with achievement is that it always feels as if you will be happy or fulfilled or fill-in-the-blank with whatever you want to feel once you get to that next milestone, if only you could just achieve that next marker. When you get there, you realize that you are excited for a little while, but it fades quickly and you regress to your normal state of fulfillment. You are left wondering why the high didn't last longer or feel stronger. When you live this way on repeat, you convince yourself that this is simply the amount of joy that you are able to feel. It resembles the experience of Sisyphus, destined to push the stone up the hill only to have it roll back down again once he reached the summit, trapped in a cycle of fruitless labor.

Every time in my career that I have started to feel out of alignment, I have instinctively relied on my gut to help guide me to the next right move. In those moments when I didn't know what I was doing, I relied on my intuition in lieu of logical answers. Every time my situation became so dire that I needed to make a turning-point decision, I sat quietly with my thoughts for days, weeks, or even months until I simply knew my next move. I have never regretted an iota of my turning-point decisions. The lesson I learned as the high-achieving introvert: I have the answers that are right for me, no one else.

CHAPTER 5: THE BOARD ROOM (FEELING SMALL)

"Your playing small does not serve the world. There is nothing enlightened about shrinking so that other people won't feel insecure around you."
– Marianne Williamson

The board room has been training grounds for feeling small in my world, because I'm usually the youngest person, the only woman, and most likely the shortest person in the room. In my very first board room meeting, I sat down in the giant chairs that are inevitably set to the perfect height for a six-foot three-inches businessman, scooted back in the seat, and found my feet dangling off the front of the chair, unable to touch the ground. This made me feel like a child, so I pulled out whatever rocket ship engineering skills I had to casually pull on random levers in an effort to adjust the chair lower, so my feet weren't dangling. Now, in a classic move of overcompensation, my chair sank quickly to the lowest setting and, voila, my feet could now touch the ground, except now I was sitting with the table up to my chest. I thought to myself, "It would have been better to have left the chair. No one could see my legs, and now I look like a lost child and I feel just as small." Since I don't have a PhD in chair science, I didn't know how to adjust it back up, so I left the chair as it was while the other senior leaders entered the room wondering who brought the child to work today. I did my best to sit up tall and fill the extra space with emphatic hand gestures.

At five feet three inches, I have often had people comment about my short stature or ask to speak to the "real" manager, inevitably because I looked too small, too young, or too female to be running the place. My tall friends find my shoulder to be the perfect resting height for their elbow, which I don't mind because I know it can be just as hard to be tall as it is small.

But how big we are on the outside does not necessarily correlate with how big we feel on the inside. Although people's explicit comments bring the idea of size to the forefront sometimes, "feeling" small is a different thing entirely. It is as if you realize that you are too exposed for your liking and you want to retreat back to where it is safe. You feel the need to fold inward, to take up less space, or to be less conspicuous. You want to ignore your needs, to allow someone else's to grow (as if they couldn't both grow together). Feeling small is a byproduct of shame, the feeling that you don't deserve something or aren't good enough to experience something as grand as what you had imagined.

The board room is not the only place I have felt as small as Alice after drinking the shrinking potion, or made myself smaller for the comfort of other people. I remember a time when I had a big speaking engagement coming up and a prominent community member asked, "How did you get THAT gig?" Part of me said in my head, "By being my awesome goddam self," but the rest of me shut down, lamenting that I was so easily found out as a fraud. There was also a time when a no-bullshit advisor of mine told me two meetings in a row what I was clearly doing wrong. I was mortified that I didn't get the lesson and sufficiently act on her advice the first time. Can I crawl into my shell now, please?

And there in that collection of moments, I find a theme: people who seem larger than me make me feel small. And of course, these are all stories I tell myself about other people to deem them as "larger" than me in the first place. Perhaps they are older, more experienced, taller, or more famous than I am. They may hold positions of authority, have accomplished something on my goal list, or are just plain inspiring in their grace and approach to life. So often the people who made me feel small were the people I revered enough to allow them the space to do so.

There are definitely those people out there who have a knack for saying things with the purpose of belittling others. This is not what I am describing. Rather, people who are perfectly well-meaning humans who have no idea they just pushed a giant button are the ones who have this effect on me. And it is my button, not theirs. I am the one choosing to have a triggered reaction to feel small in that moment.

Being an introvert, sometimes it is simply in my nature to sit back and take in the conversation in meetings rather than be the dominant speaker. I had to learn to be okay with that and not allow that to contribute to feeling small in a meeting when I wasn't "holding my own" in the conversation. If I viewed participation only as speaking, then yes, I was behind. But if I viewed participation as active listening, then I won a gold medal. And in reality, if quality participation has both speaking and active listening, I could strike that balance appropriately. It was in meetings where clearly too much value was placed on speaking over listening that my bullshit meter would go berserk and I couldn't wait to leave. I hated just trying to get a word in edgewise in order to get a talking point up on the board.

Whenever I felt small, my demeanor and behavior would totally change. I would become stiff, physically clench up, and retreat into myself. I would speak less and speak only when it was painfully calculated. I felt uncomfortably exposed, as if I was on display. I noticed a difference, and I'm sure that perceptive people around me noticed, too. I didn't like who I became when I allowed myself to be small. Realizing that acting small was not true to myself, and living larger was actually more in my comfort zone, was a revelation. This meant two things: that I needed to allow myself the permission to be a listener instead of a talker without judging myself, and that I did not need to assume that I was the younger, smaller, or lesser of the parties in the room. I was an equal player.

So, what would it take to stop myself from shrinking around larger people? It meant being aware of what

I was doing in the moment and making a conscious choice to not make myself smaller. It felt odd at first and a little unnatural to be taking up more space than my normal tendency. Over time, with practice, I recognized the root of my reaction in that moment. Sometimes it meant that the other person just needed to feel big, so I released the burden on myself to think that it was me who needed to change. Sometimes, when well-meaning advice or feedback came from someone I really admired, I reframed the situation to see it from a peer-to-peer relationship instead of a bigger-smaller relationship.

I still feel a little small in any board room, with the big chairs and the coasters that are begging me not to leave a water stain from my juice box on the table. And that is okay. At least I walk in, laugh a little, tell everyone out loud that the coasters make me feel regal, and sit comfortably at the head. I adjust my chair to wherever I damn well please and spread my shit out. Really, I am only out to convince myself.

CHAPTER 6: THE BUSINESS

"Goodness consists not in the outward things we do, but in the inward thing we are." – E.H. Chapin

The time finally came for me to start my own business. Had you asked me even three years earlier if I wanted to be an entrepreneur, I would have just laughed thinking, "yeah, right!" I should have been able to see the signs, though, that it was a good career match for me. I am very independent and autonomous, don't really like to take direction from other people, and tend to take on extreme ownership for my responsibilities. I like to be a creator, not a doer of others' ideas.

I knew starting a business would be "hard" because everyone says it is, but I had a misunderstanding that it would be this hard. I (mistakenly) thought I was better equipped than most. I had run business units before, I had a Master's Degree in Business Administration, and I was responsible for much larger budgets and Profit and Loss statements in my past experiences. This should be no problem, right? It turns out that despite knowing how to run a business, I was totally unprepared for my inner gremlins to find the air they needed to unravel me.

In general, I have always felt comfortable in my own skin, with a relatively solid feeling of confidence and contentment about myself and what I bring to the table. I haven't spent much time worrying about what other people think or adjusting my position when they don't agree. I have always been extremely aware of my effect on others but have never felt the need to change who I am for anyone else. I have always been a bit of a quirk, someone who likes to hide rubber chickens in peoples' bags or who has to shop for clothes all over because no one place could supply my eclectic interests.

Running a business is hard – not because of the business acumen required to run sound operations, but because of the inner critics, the self-doubt, and the fear that come with the territory of being vulnerable and seeing if other people place value on what you are selling. It is challenging because of the double-guessing that comes with being the sole decision maker on choices that actually affect whether or not you are going to make any money at all, some money, or live up to your potential. And here I was, being crushed by the rising expectations of greatness because I didn't have anyone holding me back anymore. The weight of my own high expectations had never felt so heavy.

When I had leaders to report to, I began to unknowingly rely on their feedback, not for the feeling of pride or direction on what to do, but as an indicator of whether my work was good enough (i.e., outstanding enough that no additional work should be put into it). My 80% effort would have been more than enough in almost every instance, but I could only go "all in." My brain would have continued to expend energy to think about ways to improve something until my boss said, "Wow, this is amazing! Nice work!" That feedback signaled to my brain that it was good enough for the audience, so I could be okay with it too. When I started my business as a solo-preneur, there was suddenly a huge void in my feedback loop that I hadn't even known was there. I needed other people's approval so that I could tell myself I had done enough, and when that source of external feedback was gone, I had no one there to stop me when it was time.

The standard of excellence that I held had always pointed me in the right direction (well, in a direction, right or not). Now, I felt like the compass I had relied on for my whole life was broken, and I was floating out into the abyss like a ship lost at sea. Once I realized that perhaps my expectations of what I "should" be doing were out of line, I really struggled to know what was true, which way was up, and what new boundaries I should draw. I had always found solace in the idea that my intuition knew what to do and the answer would come to me. I am rarely indecisive, and all of the sudden I was unable to see what was true and what my obvious next step should be. It felt like losing one of my most important senses.

The fire and brimstone of starting a business for me was not anything to do with business. It was entirely internal and emotional. Much like people would tell me that parenting is "hard" (it is really flippin' hard), most of us don't understand what exactly makes it hard until we experience it. It is hard because all of the rules by which you had lived your life are suddenly thrown out the window. It is disorienting, shakes your confidence, and stunts your ability to self-assess. Somehow, this tiny baby of a business (much like an actual baby) found its way to the deepest dark spots in my brain to give me the crucible moment I needed to flourish.

Opening a business for myself was one of the first moments that really forced a change in my thinking and my behavior. In my childhood, there wasn't much to speak of as far as landmark moments that changed my life. And without those, my perspective on life didn't change. It really snuck up on me, too, maybe because the business logistics were so easy to set up or perhaps because it felt like the right thing. In my first few months of business, I felt great and confident that I was going to ride the wave as far as it took me. I assumed things wouldn't always be that easy, so I was on the lookout for some sort of business snafu like an IRS audit or a website debacle. Then, BAM! I was blindsided by the sneak attack that my head and my heart were plotting against me.

In true high-achiever fashion and staying in line with the unrealistic expectations I tend to place on myself, I had it figured out that I would have my business comfortably on track in about three months. Maybe six. Definitely by the end of the first year. At the end of the first year, I would measure my "success" and then figure out next steps. This is where the rest of the reasonable people in the world say, "That's not how this works. That's not how any of this works!" There are two problems with this assumption. First, the timeframe. Three months is definitely an outrageous expectation to build a business, and a year is barely reasonable to assume traction. Second, how you actually define success drastically adjusts whether or not you can call yourself successful at the end of any time period. As we will discuss later, my definition of success was way out of line with what I really wanted it to be. This is a place where "shoulds" and unrealistic expectations ran wild. What I SHOULD have done is checked my attitude and recognized that I was going after the completely wrong definition of success.

My business model is based on a combination of professional coaching, consulting, public speaking, and facilitating workshops. I had never been in a "sales" position before, so this was the first time that I had to figure out how to sell my business, which, as a startup, was basically selling me. I priced too low, because I was in a place of desperation and knew that the stakes were high. It started to mess with my head that now my business was deeply personal and not enough people saw the value to buy in. It became a direct reflection of my own value and the value of my work. I doubted all that I had done to get to where I was. Did I make the wrong career moves? Was it that I had fewer years of experience than most other consultants? Or was it just me? I settled on the idea that I just wasn't enough. My inner critics came for a visit, or rather, a lengthy camping trip with an overstayed welcome.

CHAPTER 7: MEET BRIDGET

Atelophobia *(Noun)*: The fear of imperfection, of not being good enough.
Origin: Greek, Atelos (imperfect)

Like many introverts, it is common for me to have a rich inner dialogue going on at any given moment. Me, myself, and I are discussing the pros and cons and wins and losses or just enjoying each other's company most of the time. It feels as if there are so many thoughts happening simultaneously that it can't possibly be just me talking. There must be a whole bunch of characters in there. (I am confident this is normal and not some manifestation of dissociative identity disorder, so no need to call in the professionals).

More often than we realize, we have inner critics hijacking the conversation. We may not even realize what they are doing, because they are just so sly about how they creep into our subconscious thoughts. We all have these inner critics, the voices that whisper inside of us to sit down or play small. It is the voice that tells you that you are not good enough, smart enough, pretty enough, or that you are just plain insufficient as you are. They try to contain us in order to keep us safe. Our inner critics are there to protect us, so they have served a purpose, of course. We can always have more than one inner critic, or gremlin, but the first of mine who I met was Bridget.

Bridget is my true gremlin, the original gangster of shit-talking me into feeling like I should be better or more of something. She is always worried about "what if," and she makes sure to avoid sudden moves at all costs. Bridget just cares so much about me that she has always tried to be the protector, much like a young girl who smothers a bunny she caught because she is just trying to love her. Bridget is stout, small, and a little chubby, the girl with her feet dangling off the front of the chair when she sits all the way back. Bridget is named after the character Bridget Jones of the diary fame, because, with a little help from Mark Darcy, she learns to love herself just as she is.

Bridget was there back when I was in high school, when it seemed really important to get perfect grades and join clubs and prep for college. She was there in college when I applied for scholarships and when I didn't get accepted into an elite business group. Bridget enjoyed coming to work with me for my whole career when I felt like a fraud and was waiting to be "found out" that I wasn't as good at my job as the important people had thought. And she sat in the front seat when I started my own business and told me her opinion that I should do more, be successful faster, and save the world in about six months or less. She is the worst type of friend, always hanging around but never all that helpful.

Since Bridget had been a part of my thoughts and feelings for what seemed like always, I had no understanding that it was, in fact, a choice for her to be in my life. I took it for granted that she was there, and that was how it had to be. It never occurred to me that I could just let her go.

Letting go of our inner critics is hard, right? They were put there for a reason, a protective layer around our hearts to safeguard us from great loss. But here is the thing: when we shut off our ability to process great loss, it shuts off our ability to process anything that large, which means we also lose the ability to experience the greatest joy.

Now, Bridget had been with me as long as I can remember, and I had no template on how to live my life without her. Since the unknown is terrifying (especially for a planner and thinker like myself), I would always rather keep her around as a known evil before I risk utter failure in the abyss of the unknown.

But, it was time to let Bridget go.

It took me 34 years to realize Bridget was there, and once I knew, it took six more months to shake her off. It took a lot of coaching for me to finally give Bridget a proverbial hug, thank her for her help, and tell her that I could take it from here. I liken it to Marie Kondo, a famous Japanese organization expert, and her method of decluttering. In her Konmari Method, or Kondo-ing, belongings are acknowledged for their service and thanked before being discarded if they no longer spark joy. Since Bridget was no longer of service to me, I sincerely thanked her for all that she had done and told her, "I've got this." I imagined that she was relieved to be able to stop working so hard and was happy to take on a role of support instead of personal defense.

My old pal Bridget is still around, and she always will be, just with a different job now. I suspect that she misses her old job from time to time, because I catch her trying to practice her former craft. Currently, she is silently eating cupcakes in the back seat of my mental car. Sometimes she tries to climb in the front seat, but I block her and say, "No thank you, that seat is taken, and you can kindly sit your ass down in the back." She was only allowed to come on the ride if she agreed to stick to her new assigned job of supporter and cheerleader, not joy-sucker or fear-monger.

There is a difference between these two ideas: "I did something stupid" and "I am stupid." The gremlin is the latter, the internalization that *you are not enough ever*, rather than your *actions were not enough in that situation*. You give in to the inner critic when you hand over the value you have for yourself. Bridget is the embodiment of "I am not enough." As soon as I could clarify the difference between something I did and something I am, it allowed me to dissociate from Bridget. Was I doing enough in my career, my life, and my business? Once I could confidently answer yes, I could see the argument that I myself was not "enough" no longer held up.

Bridget and I were getting better acquainted before I realized that there were other people in the room with us. In fact, I had lived my whole life with Bridget before even noticing her. Who else had I yet to meet? I began to listen for what other voices might be speaking in the rich inner dialogue in my head, and as a result, learned more about the complex and varied characters I had subconsciously been collecting and carrying with me through life.

CHAPTER 8: THE BOARD OF DIRECTORS

"'You have some queer friends, Dorothy,' she said. 'The queerness doesn't matter, so long as they're friends,' was the answer." – L. Frank Baum

As I shared in the previous chapter, I am increasingly aware of the discussions going on in my head, as if the many sides of my brain are all having a rich discussion weighing all angles of every situation (again, not in a concerning way). I call this group my Board of Directors.

We all have the inner critics, the voices that whisper inside of us to sit down or play small. They try to keep us contained in order to keep us safe. The first member of the Board of Directors I met was Bridget. But they couldn't all be bad, right? I started to listen for all of the voices instead of just the ones shouting or saying negative things. What I found was that some of the board members were parts of me that I really liked, had forgotten about, or would have liked to hear more from. Each of them, even the critics, served a purpose and were in place to help me, but subconsciously I had given precedence to Bridget and some of the other naysayers. The Board of Directors is a queer bunch of friends. Would you like to meet them too?

Bridget – The Doubter
Awkward, plays small, not good enough, who let her in anyways?

You've already met Bridget. She is my true gremlin, the inner critic voice talking me into feeling like I should be better or more of something. She is always worried about "what if," and she makes sure to avoid sudden moves at all costs. I am not sure how she even gained access to the room, much less elected to the board, considering that no one likes to be around her all that much. Every once in a while, she leads a Board meeting like it's her job, and everyone leaves feeling frustrated but too polite to tell her to sit the hell down.

Bridget and I were getting better acquainted before I realized that there were other people in the room with us. In fact, I had lived my whole life with Bridget before even noticing her, so the fact that other Board members joined us in a matter of months seems like a rather progressive timeline.

During a time period when Bridget went on an extended sabbatical after I told her to get off my continent, I began to feel rather great about the fact that I was off living my best life and not even worried about the future, the unknowns, or if I was making the "right" moves. Then I met Nigel.

Nigel – The Responsible One

British, middle-aged man in a tweed jacket and bowtie. Proper, right, shouldy, realist, theorist.

Nigel is the responsible one. He looks like a balding man with glasses, a bowtie, and a tweed jacket, the kind with elbow patches that are a bit worn out but still wearable. He spends most of the day at the library researching and even packs his lunch in a sensible brown paper bag each morning so that he isn't interrupted by frivolity or joy at midday. He seems to still be adjusting to his bifocals, because he oscillates between making faces that express either disapproval or surprise. He loves to confirm anything and everything with as much data as possible to back up the theory, like an insurance underwriter unwilling to take risks. He overuses words like "should" and "realistic" and sucks all the fun out of the room. He does smile sometimes, but usually only when things feel really buttoned up.

Nigel often steps in to promote guilt when I make a large purchase ("what if I should have saved that money?") or stare with a disapproving glance when my inner child comes out ("people won't think I am very professional if I drink a juice box in the meeting"), and he doesn't seem to understand why kids these days think they can have everything without all of the hard work and "putting in the hours" that it takes to get there.

After meeting Nigel, and being old pals with Bridget, I couldn't help but wonder who else was there I wasn't aware of. I began to poke around and look for new clues. It also occurred to me that there had to be some other kick-ass people on the Board of Directors, so who were they? And they can't all be company as shitty as Bridget and Nigel, right? I went on to investigate and discovered the rest of the Board.

Chris – The Cool, Confident One
Comfortable in own skin, put together, effortless, poised.

Chris is pretty, although I'm not sure that she is aware of that. She is comfortable in her own skin, a sort of cool confidence that sometimes comes off as aloof, but most recognize it as just self-contentment. She is always well pressed, like a J. Crew model, and seems to have effortlessly put her outfit together with some things she found lying around. She is the type of friend who knows the right thing to say and the right greeting card to send at the right time. In fact, I am sure she picked out birthday cards for her people for a full year and just sent them out when the time was right with ease. She invites different groups of friends to parties and is the glue that brings others together. She listens intently to others, nodding and responding carefully once everyone has had a chance to speak. Chris makes you feel special when you are with her and perhaps also a little self-conscious.

When I watch Chris, she moves around the room not seeking anyone's approval for anything. She likes what she likes, and that is the end of it. She doesn't speak often in meetings, but when she does, everyone stops to listen because it is always good. Sometimes people think she is aloof when they don't know her or see her in passing, because she appears a little unapproachable. But once people get closer to her, they realize that she is as approachable and empathetic as they come.

Michelle – The Force to be Reckoned With

Intelligent, fierce, grounded, overcomes obstacles, convicted, authentic, above reproach, positive relationships.

Michelle graduated from Harvard, and she reads from all different sources and topics in a way that could slay even the most challenging cocktail party banter. She is unapologetically herself, but that is not to say that others' criticisms don't hurt her feelings. It's just that she knows she will not react but will inevitably walk the higher ground. She had a tough start, but her parents taught her about resiliency and overcoming obstacles, and so she flies higher every time. She picks the right battles and goes "all in" to make change in the areas that really matter. She wears sleeveless dresses (because she doesn't care what old, white conservative men in pressed khakis have to say about it) and is in high demand to sit on other Boards. She probably realizes that we are 5% intimidated by her but 95% in awe.

Michelle is the perfect balance of fierce and friendly. She serves as a role model for younger women everywhere and is the person we would all love our daughters to be when they grow up.

Steve – Technical Support
Strategic, organized, chess player, planner, identifies ripple effects, left-brained.

Steve is a born strategist who prefers to navigate himself on the road with maps rather than relying on GPS to tell him a way. He often plays open chess matches in the park and strategically lets the kids win, but teaches in ways that make them better. He prefers to have meeting agendas ahead of time, so he can prepare his thoughts. He sees how things affect one another and can visualize the big picture. Steve studies science and the natural world, seeing beauty in the rules of nature. He is the person that we all call to think through complex problems and ask, "What am I missing?" He can see the whole problem and its detailed parts simultaneously.

When Steve comes to visit, I feel compelled to be sure to have the right kind of tea on hand. He approaches the world with questions and a curiosity that makes you feel that he is intensely interested in learning more, not interrogating. He watches the news religiously, reads several sources of information daily, and devours podcasts.

Deanna – The Feeler
Energy reader, storyteller, feels the emotions in the room, the person who makes the most eye contact.

Deanna is highly sensitive to other people emotions, and she can understand the energy that is in a room long before the participants can put a name to it. She always knows what is not being said. She communicates with stories and metaphors, helping to link our current situation to a past familiar one. She and Nigel usually have an amicable disagreement in the right way to go about something, as the yin and yang to the discussion. Sometimes Steve (the strategist) drives her nuts with logic and rules. Sometimes, she thinks, there just aren't logical reasons or rules to why we do things.

Deanna cries at commercials with puppies or children, and she refuses to watch the nightly news. She can see their whole lives and emotions flash before her eyes, and it is too overwhelming. She is the one who most trusts her instincts, especially when there is not a clear answer to be found elsewhere. She likes to quote poems, songs, and movies because they serve as a concise tie between our unconscious emotions and our familiar memories and pop culture references.

Wendy - The Creative
Dancer, musician, wearer of bright colors, beats to her own drum.

Wendy tends to move her feet and sway to the music that only she hears in a "dance like nobody's watching" sort of way. She likes to wear bright colors and bold prints that make her happy. She feels most alive and at home with her theater friends, because they are all comfortable with just being themselves. She loves to sing or dance with others in the perfect combination of her own private and personal expression, but in the proximity of friends. She is unsure of what her real hair color is and has the most interesting collection of shoes I have ever seen.

Wendy listens to all types of music and can move seamlessly between genres and decades. She knows all of the words and the artists and can give interesting trivia facts like the origins of hip hop music. Her parents were free-spirited hippies, and she takes a more modern approach. She is best friends with her inner child, and her love of macaroni and cheese and mismatched clothing makes her a favorite with kids. She makes me feel lighter and younger just being around her.

It is curious that all of these characters can exist at the same time. Some of them are unlikely friends to each other, and all of them are there to preserve some part of me. Of course, they all take the lead at different times. Some days I am compelled to wear bright colors, others I am pushing forward with unwavering force, and still others I am swimming in a pool of "shouldy" responsibility. Becoming acquainted with the company I am surrounding myself with has been an exercise in understanding myself, my complex inner dialogue, and the voices that make up the undeniable force that is the high-achieving introvert.

My Board members are a combination of all of me. The reason that these characters can exist simultaneously is that they all exist in me simultaneously. We admire people or qualities, because they are mirrors reflecting back pieces of ourselves. We just frequently don't realize them in ourselves because we are so hyper-critical. But they are there, and that is why those qualities resonate for us when we see them in others. Likewise, when we see traits we dislike in others or we find our buttons being pushed, we are reacting to what we disapprove of in ourselves. The Board of Directors makes up every bit of yourself that you love and loathe, without even realizing it.

CHAPTER 9: THE LEMON PANCAKE MONOLOGUE

"Be willing to trust your instincts, especially if you cannot find answers elsewhere." – Brian Koslow

After starting my business and feeling the weight grow heavier and heavier, I came to a crossroads. I recognized that I was on the verge of a breakthrough, but I didn't know how to get to the other side. The weight and the pressure I was putting on myself was becoming unbearable, and now I was aware of my hand in it and didn't know how to stop. In the moment that it finally struck me, and I could articulate what I was feeling, I wrote down the sentence:

I am being crushed by the rising expectations for greatness because I don't have anyone holding me back anymore.

I read it over and over again. That was some heavy shit that I needed to sort through. I reached out to my coach to prompt me on some questions to consider. She sent me a list, and I began to work through my answers one by one.

I knew this moment was big, and I needed reinforcements. So, I went to a local coffee shop, ordered a plate of lemon ricotta pancakes, and had a silent conversation with myself through my tears to unpack this new realization. This was that conversation.

What am I AFRAID will happen if I release the intense pressure and/or expectations I would have placed on myself?

That I will fail, and that it will be all my own doing. No cause, just myself. A totally preventable failure. Which makes it a double failure. Failure at doing it right, and then failure after seeing the issue and still not being able to fix it. I am afraid that I have held this pressure by myself and for myself only my whole life, and that I can't be successful without it. Inevitable failure, because failure if I keep the expectations, and failure if I don't. Scratch that … inevitable failure if I keep the pressure, and only possible failure if I let them go. And possible greatness.

What would ACTUALLY be the outcome of letting go of these overwhelming expectations?

I might fail, but it would be SO MUCH LIGHTER. Either lighter failure, or total greatness.

What would letting go of these overwhelming expectations feel like?

Confident, like leveling up, not giving a shit, being the person I want to be and the world needs me to be, allowing others to see what they are looking for in me, feeling bigger (without walls or boundaries), and open up headspace for better things.

What is my definition of success?

I do not know the answer to that. Success right now? Success in 10 years? The end game? I think I can only answer it in describing my "why." The world needs me. (That sounds audacious.) The world needs people who will listen and feel, and create change for the better of humanity. I think that I can alter the course of the world. My definition of success seems to be part of the problem. So, what is true? Success would be creating something that alters the course of the world for the better.

If I held myself to this definition what would I need to do to achieve it?

- Have faith in myself that I am doing the right thing without factual backup.

- Connect with others.

- Walk the talk.

- Live on purpose.

- Experiment in bold moves.

- Be larger.

- Be clearer on and take a firm stand on what I believe in.

I am overwhelmed looking at this list – I have a lot to do to live into the definition of success.

What would I have to give up or stop doing?

- The fear, obviously.

- Stuff that isn't a "hell yes."

- Being awkward around other humans.

- Judgement about the previous three bullet points.

- Attachment to the outcome (I am doing better with others, but not myself).

And, yet, this list somehow seems more challenging to accomplish than the first one.

What specific steps could I take to unburden myself from these intense pressures when I feel or experience them?

1. Recognize them and say, "That's interesting," and then study it like a scientist who is not attached to the outcome of the experiment (judgement free).

2. Practice a higher "hell yes" threshold.

3. Build out my manifesto – what I stand for privately and publicly.

4. Experiment in bold moves (living with purpose, being larger, overcoming fear).

This feels like I am trying to dig a tunnel to China with a kid-sized garden trowel. Like big problems with the tiniest solutions. They feel "cute."

Isn't that just the thing? All of the quotes and memes and clichés of the world hold some truth. Feeling the full weight of my problems with simultaneous awareness felt like lucid dreaming, when you are dreaming but you know it is a dream in the moment. And now the answers to all of my heavy shit were hiding in plain sight on Internet memes, coffee table quote books, and inspirational coffee mugs. Things I had thought were endearing and trite were actually rooted in true solutions for my existential crisis.

I also began to question why I was still feeling conflicted about my current work situation. I was loving my work and enjoying the flexibility and freedom that comes with being your own boss, and I was certainly aware of and consciously trying to honor my values. So, what was the problem?

Even though I felt I was in the right place with my work, I still felt funky. What the hell was my problem? I was in the best place of my life – was I not capable of being happy with anything? Jeesh. I added these two questions for myself, because it became clear to me that whenever I feel discomfort, it is attributed to being out of alignment with my values. ALWAYS.

What values am I not honoring right now?

Contribution/making a difference.

Can I sustainably honor all of my values at the same time?

It is possible, yes.

I realized that I might always place value on accomplishment and making a difference, and I had to be able to reconcile living a life of aiming to do big things and being okay when the outcome doesn't turn out as I had planned. Instead of placing value on the outcome or the accomplishment, I must shift the value to the experience of the journey. If I am detached from the outcome, it doesn't matter what happens, and the value cannot be diminished from the journey. And that is how I found a path to honor all of my values at the same time.

CHAPTER 10: THE LESSON

"I can't go back to yesterday - because I was a different person then." – Lewis Carroll

We grow in tiny bursts of new awareness that push us forward until the next new lesson comes along. Change is not always a constant flow, a steady, straight line, or a lone bolt of lightning. In reality, it is often a collection of small and stretched leaps where we bound forward with new awareness that can't be unseen. If we miss or ignore the lessons, we don't get to pass GO or collect $200. We get the lesson served back to us by the universe until we master that level.

As I gained new awareness about myself and how I placed inordinate value on accomplishment, I had a big "A-ha!" moment at first discovery. But following that took many reminders of the same new idea as I adjusted to this new rule I was trying to create for myself. And there were countless aftershocks of awareness where I realized something new about my past patterns now, that I could look back on my catalog of memories with an entirely new filter. I couldn't see those things all at once – that would be too overwhelming. It's as if I had been watching the movie of my life only in subtitles, and for the first time, I was seeing it with the complete understanding of my native language.

The lesson worth sharing from my own heroine's journey is that these ideas could save others a lot of time and energy earlier in life. If I could go back in time, what would I have wanted to know? What do I wish someone had told me (not that I would have listened)?

I would have wanted to know that my value was not dependent on how much I accomplished, that the fear of failure was inevitably worse than the actual failure, and that failure guards the door to success. I would have wanted to know that I was enough.

Failure guards the door to success.

I would go back to that young girl in high school, or maybe even earlier, and spend time really seeing her. I would point out the traps that might be lurking underneath the guise of success and high-achievement. There are countless young leaders out there who have only ever seen achievement as their path, because our culture thrives on better, stronger, and more. And of course, we don't want a society full of lazy assholes with no ambition. But I think we can take the risk and tell our high-achievers drowning in deep thoughts that they are just where they need to be and that they are enough just as they are.

I recently attended a parent-teacher conference where my three-year-old son's teacher shared with me and my husband that our son was a caring and compassionate kid who cares about other people's feelings, and that he is doing the right thing. He doesn't like to make mistakes, and they are working with him on being comfortable to try new things even if it is hard and he might mess up. I think an exact quote was, "Sometimes he is really hard on himself." He is THREE. My heart nearly shattered to hear what I now saw so clearly in myself and in my lifetime. This lesson about the value of the journey and not the outcome is important as early as this, and I am acutely aware of how I can raise my children to know what I learned for myself only later in life.

There are some critical, tangible steps that I have taken to remain close to this new mindset. I read and reread the answers to my questions in order to get used to the new idea. I adjusted my "to-do" list by removing anything that was a "have to" instead of a "hell yes." I wrote on my bathroom mirror "I am enough." I allowed myself the permission to not worry about "what if" for 90 days. When I started to feel pressure or worry about what "might" happen, I actively changed my thought to one in the moment. I started putting myself in more situations where I felt uncomfortable (in a good way), like doing more impromptu speaking and riding a bike for the first time in over 15 years. I acted as if the things I really wanted to achieve were already happening. And you know what? They did. By starting to honor this new mindset and acting accordingly, the "inevitable failure" I once felt faded to make room for potential total greatness and true alignment with what truly matters most for me.

What I have learned in these crucible moments is how I can choose my future. I now strive to do less "stuff" but to play bigger, to focus on my passions and be really good at them, and to have gratitude for the time I have left to live with the weight lifted. When I realized that fear wouldn't hold me back, it didn't. While I know the inner critics will always be there, and I will always want to achieve great things, my value is no longer attached to how much I accomplish. I now find more value in the attempt, the journey, and the experience. I know that this is all part of my curriculum to learn. And that is even better.

I didn't just have one lightning bolt moment where my life changed in an instant. This is simply the start of the story, not the full description of the work, which comes next. Awareness is the key that unlocks the door. We still have to find the courage to walk through the door and the persistence to move forward even when it feels hard or unknown. When we do the work, we level up and can explore a whole new world of lessons, experiences, and pitfalls that were previously unavailable to us.

It starts with awareness. For your own internal Board of Directors to discuss, perhaps start with three questions:

- What is your definition of success?

- How do you detach your value from the outcome?

- And what are you so afraid of?

- Enjoy the journey, and do the work.

PART II: THE WORK

"Life is simple. Everything happens for you, not to you. Everything happens at exactly the right moment, neither too soon nor too late. You don't have to like it... it's just easier if you do."
– *Byron Katie*

INTRODUCTION

"I am not afraid... I was born to do this."
– Jeanne d'Arc

People often ask me, "How did you actually change, or get to the other side?" What I can tell you is that there is no one silver bullet, no one solution that will change your life and open you up to everything you are looking for in life. Rather, it is an ongoing commitment to doing the work; a string of new, tiny, life-changing glimpses of awareness that add up to big change, when you follow the course and show up for the lessons the universe places in your path. It is okay if you miss some. They will keep coming back until you master the lesson. Have you ever had different versions of the same boss you hate even when you move from job to job trying to escape it? Or have you ever recognized a pattern in your relationships where it starts out strong and then spirals into codependency? That is the universe serving up the same damn lesson until you learn what you are supposed to from it and graduate to the next level.

When you gain new awareness about yourself and the world around you, it becomes a new dimension that you simply couldn't see before, that you cannot "un-see" now. That is really the definition of life-changing in the context of this book: a new awareness that forever changes your filter on life and, because you cannot go backward, by definition your life is changed. And it is like a video game where you have to unlock a level by collecting mushrooms, slaying the dragon, and rescuing the princess before you can enter the next world. Much of the awareness I have now would have been entirely unavailable to me a year ago, because my "A-ha!" moments build on each other and require the foundation I have already built in order for me to be ready to receive them.

How do you know if you are ready to receive the universal lessons or if you are open to gaining higher consciousness? You ask for the lessons, you listen, and you do the work. It is an art form of part stillness and listening, and part getting a giant shovel, getting your hands dirty, and digging really deep within your own thoughts, feelings, and behaviors in order to make a change. This work is critical to examine that which has been left dark or silent. The stillness and solitude are crucial to you being able to process and accept what you have uncovered. Both are necessary on your path. I see some people who are willing to sit in the quiet stillness of meditation but shy away from digging deep into the unknown landscapes within themselves. Or, there are the people who dig deep but never really process and turn the new awareness into a new way of life. This is the most glorious pattern of personal growth, resilience, and pushing beyond comfort that I have found to exist, but it is not easy. If it were easy, everyone would have done it already.

I hope that you enjoyed learning more about my story and exploring the hidden inner workings of the high-achieving introvert, but the story alone is not going to get you into action. In Part Two, I break down some of the building blocks that might be useful for transforming your own experience. These are all activities that I went through as part of my journey past fear and toward personal insight. You can use them to create stepping stones of new awareness that over time will lead you to even bigger self-discoveries. In this part, I am going to challenge you to do the work. In six months or less, doing the work and reflecting on the activities will inevitably change your view of the world. Your personal universe will feel more aware, alive, expansive, and full of possibility. I will share some new ideas that may help you on your path, as well as curate some of the best ideas that I have found from thought leaders around the world that might be helpful on your quest. Let's go slay the dragons.

ACTIVITY 1: VALUES AND VALUE

"It's not hard to make decisions once you know what your values are." – Roy E. Disney

I didn't always understand what it meant to live in accordance with values. In fact, I didn't even know this really existed in the practical sense. It seemed like something only very conservative people would say (along the lines of family values), and I simply didn't understand another way to look at it. But once I recognized that my work was not aligned with what was most important to me, I couldn't un-see it. And once you are able to recognize your values, you can take steps to realign yourself with what is important.

I can still summon up what it felt like to be so far out of alignment with what really mattered to me. For days, weeks, months, the discomfort would slowly, steadily rise, peaking every Sunday afternoon as the work week loomed ahead. On the outside, I appeared distracted and was quick-tempered with those close to me, and all of my brain's working memory was hijacked by ruminative thoughts of what I "should" be doing or what I needed to be doing. The drive to work, a cocktail of dread and anxiousness, ended with a few deep breaths in the parking lot to summon the courage for the day. I would forget to greet people, because I was so consumed with the dialogue in my head. I would turn into one of "those" people who instead of asking how someone was doing, would go straight to asking what I needed to check off my mental list. I would experience meetings where I wanted to crawl out of my skin, feeling so uncomfortable that I couldn't even find the words to articulate and express my disagreement. I hated wasting time, experiencing inauthenticity in myself and others, and completing tasks without integrity.

I can look back on those moments and recall a very specific physical response. At its worst, I literally felt the urge to jump out of my skin. My shoulders were tight and hunched, I would have frequent headaches, and my physical health was notably diminished during times of the most extreme stress.

I had been successful in my work, so why did I feel this way?

If you have ever felt this discomfort (which I imagine every single one of us has), I want you to take a fresh, non-judgmental look at what you value. Get really clear on the stuff that matters to you. And then take a second look at the times in your history when you felt the discord, the misalignment that I am describing. Which of your values were you not honoring during that time?

In an exercise of example and transparency, I want to share with you here a few of my own most important values along with an instance when I was misaligned to each value.

Authenticity

I prefer things to be real, plain and simple. For at least a year, I found myself wearing terribly boring clothes to work. For some reason, I felt the need to try and look older, appear more professional, or feel more important. I am all in support of dressing well for work, I just could have done it without stuffing my personality in a box. I wore too much black for my liking, and adorned jackets and suits that would be sure to strike up zero conversations. It was a complete departure from the rest of my closet and personality. When I realized what I was doing and how it negatively was affecting how I felt about myself at work, I needed to make a change. I donated the boring pieces or moved them to the back of the closet. I resurrected all of my fun and interesting clothes and made sure to pile them on. I focused on only wearing things that gave me joy. Colored tights? Check. Red shoes? Yes. Classic black pants? Hidden.

Integrity

I can best describe this value for me as the results needing to be outstanding, but more importantly, the manner in which they were accomplished must also be exceptional. I had one boss who definitely had the right goals, but the manner in which he wanted me to do the work, how he communicated, and the way he treated people were 100% not how I would choose to do it. As a result, I felt miserable and physically uncomfortable most of the time. I spoke my mind, held true to my values, and when nothing changed, I eventually left that job.

Contribution

I run my own company, and it is awesome. And you know? Some days are hard. I have to ask myself, what could possibly be wrong with this scenario? I am doing what I love and designing my work and life, so why do I feel discord on some days? The reality is that as my company continues to grow, I have sometimes felt that I "should" be doing even more, helping more people, or making an impact on more teams, leaders, and lives. The only value that is not being fully honored is my need to contribute on a grand scale. As a result, I reexamined how I was spending my time to ensure that a critical amount was dedicated to big goals, important projects, and things a little beyond my comfort zone. When my "goals" started becoming a list of low-level tasks, I knew it was time to adjust and make sure some next-level ideas made their way to my To-Do list.

Once you recognize that feeling of discord and misalignment, you can ask yourself in the moment, "What value(s) am I not honoring right now?" If you can master the art of asking this question and being able to answer honestly, you have unlocked the power to do something about it. And as you course correct, you will find your way back to center, and the discomfort will fade. When you know what really matters to you, you can choose to bask in it. Because you can't un-see it, right?

Shortly after I woke up to my values, I was confronted with a strength-test of my values awareness, when a headhunter contacted me about a very tempting, very important role at a company. I was intrigued, and so I interviewed for the position. It went really well, and I was invited back to meet the entire executive team for an all-day affair. My gut reaction to this invitation was annoyance, because I was not excited to spend that time traveling and meeting with the team. I immediately thought, "Wait a minute! What is wrong here? I should be excited to do this and for the opportunity!" When I realized I wasn't excited, I had to unpack why not.

I realized in that moment for the first time something not only about that opportunity but also about how I had lived my life for years without realizing it. I realized that I was not excited about this role in particular because it did not align with my values of authenticity and excellence. And then my mind was blown as I recognized that I had spent years (YEARS!) working for a company already that misaligned with the very same two values. The universe was presenting a lesson again that I had refused to see before, and this time I listened. I was not excited for this role, because I recognized that working for a company that didn't always project excellence would grate at my soul again, and it would be a big mistake. I called the headhunter immediately and withdrew from consideration.

I experienced a very physical and visceral reaction in this scenario, and it helped me gain awareness to pay attention to my gut and physical reactions, as a sign for when I am clearly out of alignment with at least one of my values. Often, the first sign you may notice that you are out of alignment is that actual physical reaction. Perhaps you have spent years ignoring those small clues, but they are there. By recognizing the physical response, you can ask yourself powerful questions to get to the root of what value is being challenged in that moment. And by having the awareness, you can change your action.

It is also important to take a closer look at where your values stem from. Did you choose your values, or were they given to you by someone earlier in life, such as your parents, your past experiences, or your religion? This is the moment when you have to make the choice to choose your values for yourself, for who you are in your life now, without regard to what others might want for you. If your values are not actually your own, doing these practices won't help you. You may also ask yourself if your values are consciously chosen, or if they are based on fear. For example, if you think that one of your values is financial stability, but it is rooted in fear of returning to your childhood when your family didn't have much, that might be a fear-based value. Find the values that are consciously adopted and based on possibility rather than lack.

Try It: Values Activity

Start by making a list of all of your values that come to mind. It may be helpful to find a full list of values (Google it) and narrow them down to ten so you don't forget any. Then, narrow ten down to five. Take your top five and assess how well you are living those values and where you might be out of alignment with them. Do a gut check that these are consciously-chosen values. What did you learn about yourself?

When you consider what your value is, what comes to mind for you? If you are like me, you may frequently place all of your value in what you do for a living, or in the results or outcomes that you achieve. For high-achievers, they can start to feel trapped by where their value is placed. As described in the article, "The Talent Curse" by Jennifer and Gianpiero Petriglieri (Harvard Business Review, 2017), society has moved from the idea that someone "has" a talent, to the idea that they "are" talented. This is a treacherous change in language, because it implies that when you "are" talented, that it is your identity and a label you must always live up to, rather than a talent that is separate from yourself that you can invoke on occasion. If we begin to place all of our value eggs in the basket that we "are" talented, that creates an immense pressure on ourselves to live up to higher and higher expectations, whether those expectations are real or imagined, our own or from others.

Elizabeth Gilbert, in her TED Talk titled "Your elusive creative genius," also discussed this phenomenon when it comes to creative work. She explained how the Greeks and Romans saw genius as something that came to visit you, not a permanent character trait.

This is where the dark corners of perfectionism and imposter syndrome breed. We are dubbed as talented, high performers, or high-potential, and suddenly we have to keep up the façade at all times. We are constantly waiting for others to find us out and discover that we are a total sham, simultaneously making every effort to prevent that discovery from happening. The problem here is two-fold: we place all of our value in who we are, and we put unrealistic expectations on ourselves by claiming we "are" talented instead of we "have" a talent.

I can remember times from very early in my career where I was labeled as a high-potential leader. Every chance I had to officially prove myself became scarier than the last, because the stakes were higher. Each opportunity to prove myself was my next big chance to be utterly exposed, and my biggest fear was that those responsible for my career would be disappointed and say, "Oh, she's not who we thought she was." Did you just catch that I said "those responsible for my career?" The joke was on me, because no one is responsible for my career except for myself, and what I was really saying to myself was "Maybe I am not who I thought I was" and "I am not good enough."

You can combat this issue for yourself by considering where you place your value. In my journey, I shared that the ultimate lesson I learned was to place my value on the journey and experience rather than the result or achievement. Once I was able to enjoy the journey for what it was and no longer be attached to the outcome, my value existed regardless of the path I took, the result it created, or what others thought of it.

Try It: Self-Value Mantras

Repeat these to yourself. Write them on sticky notes all over your home. Say them out loud.

- I am the owner of my own path.
- I am exactly who I am supposed to be.
- I am enough.
- I have many talents.
- My talents don't own or define me.

ACTIVITY 2: DEFINITION OF SUCCESS

"Success is following the pattern of life one enjoys the most." – Al Capp

Have you ever had the feeling of accomplishing something and being surprised that it didn't bring you as much fulfillment as you thought it would? I have experienced this in my own life both when things were going perfectly and when they clearly weren't. What I have come to realize is that I was operating with a definition of success that wasn't true for me. I was trying to achieve, to reach some outcome that didn't actually mean much to me, like a business objective or a key performance milestone. Instead, what if we focused all of our superpowers toward the right destination? It doesn't matter if you are in just the right place in life, or if you know some adjustments are in order. Your energy can be redirected toward the things that matter most to you by getting crystal clear about how you define success.

How Do You Define Success?

When I first considered the question "What is your definition of success?" I was stuck. I asked, "What do you mean? Success as in, a day? A year? Ten years?" I realized in that moment that how I was defining success was part of my problem. I thought success to me was getting bigger, better, and further. And my efforts were matching that. However, when I found how I really defined success, I was no longer allocating my time and energy toward the things that mattered most to me.

If I really define the type of success for myself that would bring lasting, meaningful joy and fulfillment, it doesn't have to do with climbing a career ladder, earning a bonus, or even slaying a big project at work. There is nothing wrong with those things – in fact, they feel great! I have simply found them to be short-lived wins *for me*. Sometimes we spend much of our lives, especially at work, accomplishing amazing successes yet somehow feel unfulfilled. Why is that? It is because we are expending energy on wins that don't add up to the definition of success that really matters to us.

If you start with this one question, you will be asking yourself about something that has seemed so obvious to you that you haven't even thought about it for a long time. Ask this question of yourself on the largest scale that you can muster, the type of success that lasts beyond the moment.

Nailed a project? Success! Got that promotion? Success! Didn't eat the whole pint of ice cream in one sitting? Success! Of course, these are all wins. But if you looked back over the entire course of your life, what would you need to see in order to feel a deep level of success and fulfillment? If it is money, or title, or "the chase," then great! No judgement here on the nobility of your definition of success. As long as you are honest with yourself about your true definition of success, you are on the right track. You can bring your new and clear definition to find fulfillment in what you are already doing, or to identify where to redirect your time and energy.

A principle called the Hedonic Treadmill (or Hedonic Adaptation) observes that humans eventually return to their baseline level of happiness following good or bad events. The happiness one experiences from a win or sorrow from a loss is often short-lived before returning to personal equilibrium. However, your baseline happiness level may grow as personal successes raise the bar on your own expectations. As your expectations rise for yourself based on past accomplishments, your definition of success evolves. As your definition of success progresses, it is important to check yourself to ensure that definition still remains in line with your personal truth.

Finding your Definition of Success

I used to define success in line with societal rewards. It is common for us to accept the definition of success that someone told us we should have or that we learned by gathering the context clues from what society seems to honor, like climbing the corporate ladder or going to college. In fact, I didn't realize there could be another way to define it.

I started by beginning to think of success in bigger and longer terms. In the biggest and longest litmus test, I visualized what I wanted my final thoughts to be as I died at the end of my life. Never once have I imagined in that moment that I would hope I had worked more, answered more emails, or that I had won more awards. In that moment of reckoning when it all gets summed up, I would want to know with every fiber of my being that I changed peoples' lives for the better and made a difference in the world. So that, in turn, became my purpose.

I then began to work backward from the end of life (which is hopefully many decades away) and think in smaller increments. Is what I envision twenty years from now in line with my purpose? What about what I am doing 10 years from now? Five years? One year? Right this moment?

I am willing to believe you are reading this book because some part of you knows that what you are doing right now with your life does not fully align with the truth you are looking for on your last day of life. Now is the day you can begin to make small changes toward the future you want.

Let's pause for a minute to step back into the reality of your actual current situation. You have a propensity for achievement, so of course you have had moments in your life that were big accomplishments and made you feel wildly successful in that moment. I mean, come on! We are achievement addicts – that shit feels really good. I want you to think back to a time when you felt really successful, perhaps at work. I remember times when one of the top executives of my company would come and give rave reviews for the work my team was doing. That felt amazing! It felt like winning, like total success. And it was success. In hindsight, there is a difference between that moment of feeling excited versus experiencing a feeling of long-term, lasting fulfillment. On my death bed, I will not be thinking of accolades or those short-lived shooting star moments, but I will be cataloguing whether or not I changed peoples' lives, whether the work I did mattered. If you imagine on your death bed that awards and winning will be your focus, that is perfectly normal and okay; no judgement. I am simply trying to clarify the difference between when we feel "successful" for a moment, and things that match our definitions of success for long-term fulfillment.

If I reflect on those fleeting moments of feeling successful, they do not withstand my test:

- Do they feel successful? Yes.

- Is it good work? Yes.

- Will it matter a year from now? Probably not.

- Does it alter the course of the world for the better? No.

What is my definition of success? Creating something that alters the course of the world for the better, and maintaining the life I love.

Success would be creating something that alters the course of the world for the better.

So... what's yours?

Try It: Defining Success Activity

Take a pen and paper, and consider the following questions for reflection. Write your answers in ink:

1. Create a vivid vision of you in your last day of life where you feel the most success, fulfillment, and love that you can imagine. What do you see? How do you know you have been successful?

2. How do you ensure your final day vision aligns with your vision in twenty years? 10 years? Five years? One year?

3. What is your definition of success? Is it big enough and far-reaching enough that it goes beyond your life now, the job you have now, or your immediate fulfillment?

4. Does your definition of success unwaveringly align with your personal values?

5. Would you be proud to tell yourself and others your definition of success?

6. How do you detach your value from the outcome or your accomplishments?

7. What are you so afraid of?

ACTIVITY 3: WHAT TO DO AND WHAT TO GIVE UP

"Happiness is not found in things you possess, but in
what you have the courage to release."
– Nathaniel Hawthorne

The idea that mutated from "I can do anything" to
"I *should* do *everything*" was one that moved from a
push to pursue excellence, to simply a push to pursue. In
reality, we can't do everything, and frankly, we shouldn't
do everything. Unless your life's work is to do everything
there is to do on the whole damn planet at least once,
then that would be a singular focus under which you
could argue doing everything would be a reasonable
feat. Otherwise, why on God's green earth are we all
moving around acting like we have to stuff ten pounds
in a five-pound bag and look good doing it? My new
approach is to see where I can do fewer things, choose
the things I really like, and do them with excellence.

This, of course, has not been a revelation where overnight I simply cut out half of my life and felt a whole lot lighter. I often envy those people who can dump their entire closet and stick with a capsule wardrobe of 32 clothing pieces. I am still trying to conquer that beast. Nope, this is more of a "clean the closet, feel good about it, then as more junk slowly creeps back in, repeat the process over and over until the end result is closer" type of thing.

When I realized that my own expectations for myself were spiraling out of control, I had to ask myself the tough questions on what it would look like to achieve my definition of success, and identify what exactly I was holding onto with my Kung Fu death grip that was not serving me. Here again are the two simple questions that I asked myself, and my answers:

If I held myself to this definition, what would I need to do to achieve it?

- Have faith in myself that I am doing the right thing without factual backup.

- Connect with others.

- Walk the talk.

- Live on purpose.

- Experiment in bold moves.

- Be larger.

- Be clearer on and take a firm stand on what I believe in.

My immediate gut reaction is to judge my list. I ask myself, "What the hell have you been doing this whole time then, if not this?" I have been finding a lot of stuff to keep me busy, but on any given day, I suppose I would struggle to tell you that I accomplished anything of note. The achiever side of me says, "None of those items seem to be attached to earning a promotion or a medal." The pragmatic voice says, "Those things are doable. People do these things well, every day." I realize that I can conquer this list, if I choose to, but I simply won't have time if I hold onto all of the other things that are taking up my mental processing space. So, what needs to go?

What would I have to give up or stop doing?

- The fear, obviously.

- Stuff that isn't a "hell yes."

- Being awkward around other humans.

- Judgement about the previous three bullet points.

- Attachment to the outcome (I am doing better with others, but not myself).

And, yet, this list somehow seems more challenging to accomplish than the first one. I realize by noting how hard this list seems, that I haven't really ever released anything back into the wild. Maybe I have gotten bored with things and decided not to do them anymore. But this is different. This is Kondo-ing. It is thanking something and then setting it free if it doesn't spark joy (see Marie Kondo's work).

After careful consideration, I realized that one of the key conduits to all of the beliefs I needed to give up was the fear of the future. I have never been one to ruminate on regret, but I could run "what if" marathons for the rest of my life. The "what ifs" are fear of what could happen, and fear of the future is worthy of its own chapter, which we will cover later.

Here are some tactics to decide what to keep and what to give up:

Do Only the Things That Only You Can Do

This means, if you have other people that report to you or that work with you, focus your energy on only doing the things that must be done by yours truly. Everything else can be delegated, dropped, or hired out.

As a leader: Assign someone who is not you to own all tasks. Your job is to synthesize and to follow-up. Only you can do the synthesizing and the following up. And only your team should be doing the "stuff." This may mean investing some time on the front side to teach others to be as proficient as you in those tasks (yes, I know, if you want it done right, you have to do it yourself, blah blah), but the payoff is ten-fold when you are able to free yourself up for the things that really bring you fulfillment.

At home: Decide as a home unit how to divide up the work. Sometimes I have a five-page list in my head of things that need to get done, half of which may never occur to anyone else around me. From that list I think,

"Does this even need to be done?" (drop it all together), or I ask my partner to do the things that he would probably do anyways as well as things he may not realize are on my mind. That way, I only end up doing the tasks that only I can do, not those plus all the other duties that double the list. Also, I delegate and pay someone to do things that make sense, like clean my house every other week.

In your business: Can you hire a virtual assistant, an intern, or even someone who costs less per hour than you do, who can do it in half the time? Then WORTH it.

See the Alternative in Technicolor

One way to get comfortable with moving toward a new reality is to actually hear, see, feel, and taste it. If you can start to view the future state as if it is really happening, it quickly seems more attainable. It would be as if instead of rebuilding a whole engine to a car, you look in and realize that with a few wrench turns, tune-ups, and a quart (gallon?) of fluid, it is as if you have a whole new car.

Ask yourself questions to create a vivid vision of what the alternative would look like in real life. Here are some visioning questions that I asked myself during my own moment of truth:

- What would ACTUALLY be the outcome of letting go of these overwhelming expectations?

- What would letting go of these overwhelming expectations feel like?

- What would you do differently when you were free of your overwhelming expectations?

- What do others notice about you in this new place?

- What do you notice about yourself?

I truly believe, and have seen the evidence with my own eyes, that we are only one new awareness away from changing the rest of our lives.

Try It: Visioning Activity

Write a one-year and five-year vision for yourself. Write everything in the present tense, as if it is actually already happening. Write all sentences in a positive tone (for example, instead of "I am no longer scrounging for money," write "I am living in an abundant world and have everything I need.") Your vision should be so detailed that it invokes all of your senses and is vivid when you try and see it. Ask yourself what you notice about this new world you created and what has changed. Also be aware of what is not present, as these are perhaps things you do away with in your life now.

ACTIVITY 4: LEVELS OF LISTENING

"Think with your whole body." – Taisen Deshimaru

To support the goal of creating connections with others, I isolated one of the most critical elements of good communication: listening. Communication is simply one of the biggest factors in our relationships. It is a critical element in our work connections, how we see our boss or company leadership, and how we grow (or break) personal relationships. And one of the most critical skills needed is, in fact, not saying anything at all. Those who are introverts do not need to be told this, but perhaps it helps to hear a reminder that everyone has the permission to listen and be quiet.

There are several levels of listening that you may practice, some of which are not serving you. If you recognize that improving your communication would be valuable, then having awareness of how you are listening to others and yourself will help you. And let's be honest, every one of us could benefit from stronger communication. I have yet to see an organization that did not list communication as one of the key drivers to improving employee engagement.

The three levels of listening here can help you determine how well you are communicating with others.

Level 1: Listening to Respond

Do you ever find yourself listening to someone with the sole purpose to respond? If you are crafting what you are going to say back in response while someone is speaking, then you are practicing Level 1 listening. It is about you, not the other person. Unless you drop the need to make it about you, you won't be able to achieve deeper listening. This happens frequently when two people are arguing their opposing political views. They put energy into making their point instead of listening to the other's view and adjusting their response to match what they hear. Most listening happens at this level.

Simply put: You are doing too much talking, and you are making it about you.

Level 2: Listening to Hear

This is when you are listening to really hear the words the other person is saying. You respond only after you've processed what's been said, and it is now about the other person, not you. This helps you start to understand at a higher level, and it helps the other person begin to feel heard. You are proving that by being able to paraphrase back what the other person just said. This is effective listening, but you might be missing some other conversational cues.

Simply put: You are hearing the words and focusing on the other person. Good work.

Level 3: Listening to Feel

If you are deeply listening, you can not only hear what the other person is saying but can also feel what they feel and intuitively hear what isn't being said. While you might not spend every meeting deep in this level of listening (it takes commitment and presence), this can be a valuable skill to sharpen with your most important relationships. As a result, the other person will truly feel heard and understood. Since our closest relationships are often the ones we take for granted, practice this with your team, your partner, or your children to find maximum impact.

Simply put: You can hear and feel more information and can better provide empathy and connection to others.

Some naturally intuitive people (INFJs and the like, I am talking about you) and many coaches I know spend a significant amount of time in Level 3 listening. If you are normally in this space, it can be exhausting sometimes to take on so much information about the other person for long periods of time. It is important to be aware of, and choose, when to use each level.

Listening to Yourself

Each of us has a different capacity for listening, but, to be sure, it is a muscle that we can train over time. As an introvert who relies heavily on intuition, it is my natural tendency to focus on listening more than talking. There are even times that I have done a fine job ignoring myself, or ignoring my gut. But in retrospect, I cannot really think of a time when following my gut steered me wrong. If it had, it clearly didn't make a big enough impact for me to remember. I do know that all of my biggest mistakes can be traced back to not listening to my gut. Every. Single. One.

For introverts, it can sometimes be challenging to quiet the rich inner monologue and really tune into what your intuition is telling you. We often make a lot of rules, interpretations, assumptions, and stories for ourselves, many of which may not be true, or your intuition speaking. And many introverts have strong intuitive natures already. Whenever I made a big mistake, I had an initial intuitive reaction and then talked myself to death with all of the reasons and "facts" as to why I should do something other than my intuitive response. Usually, these reasons are full of meeting other peoples' expectations and a whole lot of "shoulds."

Try it: Listening Activity

Keep a log of your interactions for a full day to track who you spoke with, what level of listening you used, and why you listened at that level. Identify what caused you to be distracted and listen at Level 1 with one person, and why you listened deeply with another. Look at the trends in your log: how much time did you spend at each listening level? How did each one feel different to you? What could you do to be a more effective listener tomorrow? Make it an experiment, review your results, and try again the next day. You can improve your listening muscles in a matter of days.

For extra credit and to tap into your own intuition, keep a similar log of your interactions with yourself of when you listened to yourself, when you felt something but ignored it, and when (in hindsight) you didn't pause to reflect on your thoughts or feelings at all.

After you track it for some time, can you figure out just how much your level of listening, either to yourself or to others, is costing you? It could be costing you time, money, jobs, or friends. Or worse, joy.

ACTIVITY 5: FEELING "ENOUGH"

"What is really hard, and really amazing, is giving up on being perfect and beginning the work of becoming yourself." – Anna Quindlen

In an earlier chapter of the book, you met Bridget, my inner critic who tells me "I am not enough." She still hangs around now and then but stays in the corner and rarely overstays a very short welcome.

Have you figured out who your inner critic voice is yet? Have you imagined them as a real person and named them? Believe me, this is the first step to removing them from power. You should be able to close your eyes and picture in exact detail what your inner critic looks like and sounds like. I almost picture it like the movies, "A Beautiful Mind" or "Fight Club" when the main character has someone they see lurking in the corner of the room who is really just a figment of their imagination. Well, you know, without the whole actual hallucination thing.

Release Your Inner Critic from Their Post

When something has been with you for so long, it can be hard to let go. And trust me, your gremlin voice is going to fight to stay alive and won't always just go quietly into the night. You have to really be ready to break up with your inner critic. In order to be ready, you have to have already named them, personified them, and become more aware when they are lurking. This is an important step in the process to be able to see your inner critic as a character outside of yourself, not part of you. Once you are aware and used to them being there, eventually they will wear out their welcome. This is the time when you ask yourself, what purpose is the critic serving in your life? You subconsciously put it there for a reason, and it is often there to protect you from something. So, what is it? This process of awareness in itself takes a little time.

Once you realize that your inner critic has worn out their welcome, it is time to release them from their post. Think of a new job the inner critic could be doing where their energy is used for good rather than stopping you. What new service could be a better use of your inner critic's skills and energy? I liken this to when your toddler or an annoying relative just wants to help in the kitchen. Instead of being annoyed at them messing up your kitchen, give them the task to chop all the onions in the corner. BAM - their zeal to be a part of the tasks is channeled in a helpful way.

Since we want the inner critic to be released for good, you have to have a chat with them about their new gig. You have to be the one that gives them permission to go be of use elsewhere. Here is the conversation that I had with Bridget when it was time to say goodbye:

> Me: You know, Bridget [gives hug], I want to thank you and acknowledge you for all of the time and energy you have spent with me. And at this time, you are not needed for this next phase that I am about to walk. I will take it from here.
>
> B: [Cries a little, hugs me tighter, afraid to let go.]
>
> Me: Since I no longer need you to protect me from all of the scary things that might happen to me in the future, I was hoping you could instead help me in a different area. I would like for you to cheer me on when I am feeling unsure or need a boost. Do you think you could do that instead?
>
> B: [sniffling] Yes, I would love to if it means I don't have to go away. I have just been waiting for you to ask me! Can I have some pom-poms?
>
> Me: [Sigh of relief] Yes, Bridget, you can have pom-poms.

My awareness of Bridget's existence and lurking doesn't go away. I can't unsee her. However, now, I envision Bridget as one of the Saturday Night Live cheerleader characters giving "the Perfect Cheer," or I picture her as a friend I am looking for in the crowd at a race to cheer me on while I am running. This is the big sign I always envision Bridget is holding during my race:

What about the other members of the Board of Directors? The ones who weren't serving me well received a similar sendoff to the one Bridget received. The lovely and helpful ones got to keep their jobs, and with the naysayers gone, they had the room they needed to flourish. The Board members that represented creativity, poise, empathy, and confidence were allowed to stay, and for the first time in my life, I had to appreciate and accept the lovely parts of me that I had undervalued for so long.

I now actively try and define what my superpowers are, and when I admire these qualities in others, consciously recognize that these qualities I hold in high regard in others are actually those that I see within myself. The next time you admire someone, write down all of the things that you appreciate about them. You will be amazed, if you are willing, to see every last one of those qualities in yourself.

What Would It Take to Feel Enough?

What would it take for you to feel "enough?" To feel complete? Have you ever really asked yourself this? What would actually need to happen for you to feel this way? Much like clarifying your own definition of success, you may look at what you need to feel "enough," and it only takes some simple ingredients, like love, trust, or understanding. Of course, there are times when we seek love and understanding from those close to us, but more often than not we are the ones holding back the love and understanding that we need from ourselves. Which is great to realize, because it means that we are fully capable of giving that to ourselves without anyone else's doing!

Sometimes there are people in our lives who trigger our self-questioning about feeling enough. For me, these were often people who felt larger than me, and in many cases, people who I really admired or whose opinions I cared a lot about. Knowing who these people are and why they trigger you can be helpful in preventing yourself from shrinking smaller around them. When people push our buttons, though, we must remember that they are OUR buttons, not theirs. It tells us something about ourselves. For people who felt larger but I didn't admire and respect, I simply removed them from my view. For those who I admired and wanted to keep around, I reminded myself of what triggered me when I saw them and mentally prepared myself to be enough just as I was – no shrinking necessary.

That is what it takes for me to feel like enough: simply love and understand myself. Your answer might be different. It is your own path. Just don't overlook the simplest or most obvious answer if you are willing to see it. And that is giving something to yourself.

Try It: Write "I Am Enough," and Say It Out Loud

Write down "I am enough" in big, bold letters somewhere visible. Easy, fast, and yet, you haven't done it. Why? Because it is weird to see it written down or maybe because you don't want others to see that you need that reminder, and you are trying to look like you've got it together all of the time. That hasn't helped you so far, so just try it.

I write messages in window markers (or dry erase markers) on my bathroom mirror. You could use post it notes or print out a giant page that you decorated on your computer, whatever it takes. Every time you see it, I want to you read it out loud. It will be strange at first to hear yourself saying it, but the fact is your brain doesn't really recognize the difference between if you actually believe it yet or not. You are reading it, saying it, hearing it, and subsequently internalizing it. Eventually, the phrase won't seem so foreign or so inaccurate as when you first wrote it down.

Finally, tell others about it. Since it is in a visible spot, eventually someone else will notice it. (If they don't, it means you tucked it in page 60 of your planner, and you didn't do the assignment). Tell someone about your inner critic, what her name is, and how she has been reassigned. Thank them for asking, and share a goal that you are working on. Picture your inner critic cheering you on to that goal instead of holding you back.

ACTIVITY 6: FEAR OF FUTURE

"Nothing in life is to be feared, it is only to be understood." – Marie Curie

I have found through coaching many high-achievers, as well as reflecting on my own experiences, that many of the feelings of anxiety or feeling trapped have to do with fear of one thing in particular: the future. When we feel shame and regret, we are ruminating on the past and what we wish we would have done differently. But when we feel fear and anxiety, that is trepidation in anticipation of what might happen in the future. If we are planners and thinkers, as many introverts are, then we can expend an inordinate amount of energy considering all possible future outcomes, identifying worst-case scenarios, and attaching fear and anxiety to what *might* happen if we let our minds run amuck.

I frequently felt fear of the future. In fact, I was trapped in it. I was always waiting to be found out, for the other shoe to drop, and for the bottom to fall out of my successes. I would worry as a parent that my child could get hurt or would fret that a contract would fall through. It became an out-of-control cycle where my brain would assume that because my three-year-old son wasn't toilet training yet that I would inevitably have to move him into his college dorm in diapers, and then he would never meet a nice girl because he was still in diapers, and I would be stuck with him living in my basement playing video games alone as a 35-year-old man. And I vouch that this is a normal human reaction, but I could just save myself all of the stress and worry and trust that it will solve itself.

Here are a few methods of letting go of the fear of the future, or the fear that stops you from taking forward action. Since different things work for different people, you might find one of these resonates for you more than others.

The 5 Second Rule (Mel Robbins)

Mel Robbins, author of "The 5 Second Rule," describes how we often have instincts or urges to take action, but within five seconds our brain will try and convince us otherwise and derail our initial plan. This comes from fear of what might happen – fear of the unknown – and is your brain's way of protecting you from something that is out of your norm. When you are faced with an urge to act, count "Five, four, three, two, one" and then physically move in some way. This gets your brain to move forward and counteract that subconscious automatic shutdown we usually experience.

Pre-Traumatic Growth (Sheryl Sandberg and Adam Grant)

After Facebook COO and author Sheryl Sandberg's husband unexpectedly died in 2015, her journey back to joy through resilience was the impetus for her second book, Option B, which she co-wrote with psychologist and Wharton professor, Adam Grant, Ph.D. In conducting research for this book, the concept of post-traumatic growth came up as they saw time and time again that there was often positive personal growth that came out of traumatic situations. People embraced more gratitude, strengthened relationships with friends and family, or started living life to the fullest following a traumatic incident or loss. So, Sheryl suggested, why can't we have pre-traumatic growth? That way we can make a list of all of the things that might go wrong and then check for those things in advance to prevent them, or even begin practicing gratitude before a crisis.

If we take time to examine and better understand what might go wrong, perhaps it is not nearly as bad as we thought it might be. Or, we might realize that everything in our control is being mitigated, and everything out of our control is simply that, out of our hands, and isn't worth worrying over anyways.

Fear-Setting (Tim Ferriss)

Speaking of making a list of possible failures to prevent and check...

In 2017, Tim Ferriss delivered a TED Talk on the main stage about fear and introduced the idea of "fear-setting." It is the practice of defining your fears, planning in advance what can be done to prevent them, and should they actually occur, what can be done to repair them. By doing this planning, it takes the mystery out of what could happen, and it diminishes its power to make you feel afraid of the unknown.

We often fear the future in a way that turns out to be much worse than what actually happens in reality. Either we assume a worst-case scenario and that doesn't turn out to be true, or our anxiety over what we think may happen is grossly inflated compared to if that thing actually happened. That means that a lot of the anxiety we create for the future is our own and unnecessary.

To complete fear-setting, Tim suggests that you make a list of all of the things that you are afraid of. Then, write what can be done to prevent them in the next column. In the third column, write what you would do if that fear actually happened. Now, you have a plan.

Beyond these tactics of reducing the fear of the future, focusing your energy around the present can also stave off this curse. By focusing on and fearing future states, we rob the present of the attention that it deserves, and the time spent with the joy of now. Here are some ways that you can stay focused in the present (more about these topics can be found in Activity 10 as well).

Meditation and Centering

Yogis and spiritual practitioners have long touted the physical, mental, and emotional benefits of meditating, but in recent years, science has actually begun to support those claims with data. Sara Lazar, a neuroscientist at Harvard Medical School, ran a study finding that meditation reduces stress, helps you think more clearly, and can literally change your brain over time. But even without eons of practical application and new-fangled science data, just trying a meditation practice that you actually stick with will likely be enough to convince you of the benefits.

If you are new to this space, employ some tools to help. Use a meditation app, like Headspace or Stop, Breathe & Think, for guided mediation. Find a one-minute centering exercise that is only a Google search away. When you are feeling frazzled or unfocused, even a few minutes of this can help bring you back to center.

Intention Setting

Your meditation or centering time is a great opportunity to set an intention for the day, or for a certain activity. Your intentions should be true to you in the present, not focused on something you "should" do in the future. No need to judge your intention if it is big enough, noble enough, or anything enough. If you don't know where you are going, any path will do. Set the intention to get you traveling in the right direction.

Mindfulness Exercises

What I enjoy about mindfulness exercises is that you can practice being mindful while doing damn near anything. You can practice mindfulness while you eat (savoring each bite rather than wolfing down an entire plate of pancakes without even tasting them), have a conversation, or even while you're driving. Like any meditation or activity in being present, it is a muscle that can be strengthened through practice. Doing it more and more while studying the outcome like a scientist (i.e., not being attached to the outcome) can help you see the benefits of building the muscle.

Allowing for Blank Space

Much of our frenzy comes from trying to shove too much into too little time. In a world that seems to glorify being busy, it can feel unproductive and slacker-ish to create blank space on your calendar, take breaks, or allow for your mind to wander or dabble in creativity. This premise is utter bullshit.

Particularly for high-achieving introverts, we are caught between the crux of always doing more and also needing some solitude to recharge our batteries. When I worked in busy corporate roles, I was most successful when I had buffer time built in between meetings, even if it was 10 minutes, to just sit in silence. It was like plugging in your phone for just 10 quick minutes to charge it enough to get through the next hour. I would create closure from the last meeting, prepare thoughts for the next meeting, and with any time remaining, troll around on Twitter.

I will go more in depth on ways to be in the present in later chapters, but the end goal here is to focus on the present in order to wipe out our fear of the "what ifs." Begin making the change by recognizing fear of the future, and then bring it back to what you will do in the present. Additionally, you may notice that most of these solutions have to do with doing less, not more. Once you are aware of your future-oriented fears (no matter how small), you can understand them, plan around them, and declutter them altogether.

Try It: 90 Days Fear-Free

Try it for 90 days, and love it, or your money back. I'm kidding, you did it for free.

In all seriousness, allow yourself the permission to live without fear of "what ifs" for 90 days. Whenever you feel fear of the future creeping in, replace it with a different thought that honors the present. You won't be perfect at first, but watch over time to recognize that when you let go of fears, either the thing you feared never really happened, or it did but wasn't nearly as bad as your mind made it out to be. Assess how this feels after 60 or 90 days. What feels different when you release your fear of "what if"?

ACTIVITY 7: SHOWING UP WHEN YOUR ASSIGNMENTS COME

"In the depth of winter, I finally learned that within myself there lay an invincible summer."
– Albert Camus

I am a firm believer in the universe and the role it plays in our lives. I am not a religious person, but I am a spiritual one, so rather than ascribing to any particular religion or specific higher power, I suppose you could say that the universe is the closest thing. I see it as a kind of ecosystem. Bigger than any one person, it operates on its own laws versus the teachings of one man or woman. As with any form of faith, we often have to experience something that leads us to confirm our belief, and I have tested and confirmed my faith that there are unseen forces working around me on more than one occasion.

I have often found that when the universe has something that we need to learn, it presents opportunities to learn it. If we are not tapped in to listen and learn, we may ignore it or miss it completely. Think back in time. Have you ever had a boss that you hated, so you quit your job only to find that same person reincarnated in a new boss somewhere else? Or you left a job that didn't align with your values only to take a new job that also didn't align, and then rinsed and repeated? Or perhaps you became sick or broke a bone as a forced message to slow the hell down? Yep – that is the universe shaking you firmly by the shoulders until you show up for your assignment.

I will share with you a few lessons that had to be presented more than once for me to get it. I wrote earlier in the book about realizing after interviewing for a big Human Resources role that it did not align with my values; I wasn't truly excited about the opportunity beyond the big responsibility, growth potential, and matching salary. It took me this job interview experience to realize that I had already lived that lesson. I spent years before that in a company that was equally out of alignment with my values. I didn't get the message the first time, and the universe had to tempt me with a lucrative opportunity for me to recognize the lesson I had already experienced. In another example, I spent many months being miserable in more than one role because I felt really oppressed by the direction that I had to take from others. I really loved making the strategy and then having the runway to execute on it. This had to be presented to me a second time before I realized that my path was actually to become an entrepreneur, where I set the strategy and made the decisions without answering to anyone.

I have been lucky in that the universe has not had to club me over the head with my assignments. Usually it was a lesson I experienced but didn't learn the punch line for, and a second opportunity was the push where I actually learned the lesson in hindsight. I attribute my relative success here to my innate intuitive capabilities. I have always been very intuitive, with a strong gut reaction that shouts loud enough to follow. And that still doesn't mean I always followed it. I had numbed my ability to sense what was really important for me for years, because I was so definitively on the path toward my old definition of success and accomplishment. If my intuition was talking during most of that time, I wasn't listening. Surely, I would pay attention to avoid dark alleys or danger, but never to stray off of my path of success. I remember being in college when I first learned about Life Coaches. I was amazed that this was an actual career, and even knowing practically nothing about it, I said to myself, "That is what I am meant to do." At the time, I was studying to be a Finance major with honors and had a whole plan laid out to work in international finance, wearing really nice suits and traveling to Europe a lot. My message to myself became, "If I wasn't doing this, THAT is what I would be doing." As the universe would have it, I figured out before I graduated that I did not want to jet set with fancy bankers' suits (my first step back into alignment to my true self), but I did not decide to go be a professional coach for at least ten more years.

One interesting side effect that I have noticed with paying closer attention to my intuition and emotions, is that my ability to experience emotions (and intuition) has expanded in all directions. It is normal for us to try and dull pain that we feel or to get rid of it all together.

I have allowed myself to feel and work through deeper pain rather than try and push it away, and as a result, I have experienced deeper joy and other emotions in all directions. It feels like watching *The Wizard of Oz* in its original form and then switching to the HD, digitally remastered version. By listening and allowing, you can begin to experience life in technicolor.

Tapping into Intuition

When we begin to pay closer attention to our internal thoughts and feelings, our physical state, and our intuitive "gut reactions," we become more available to capturing the signals our intuition is sending to us. I have found that when I am very busy and do not have enough alone time and space for reflection, or have too much mental load stuck in my working memory at once, I have no space left to listen to intuition. It's as if my senses are dulled, and I block it out. But when I have more space, I find that I have more intuitive hits. Often, they come in the form of these types of statements:

- "I am not sure why, but this just came to mind…"

- "Something just came to me…"

- "An idea just hit me…"

- "I just have a feeling about this…"

That is it! For basic intuitive information, that is how it shows up. You don't have to be a psychic, an oracle, or a Zen monk to listen to intuition. It may simply require pausing after you hear yourself make one of these types of statements and listening to what it is saying.

Think back to how many times you have said one of those statements to yourself, and your brain immediately rationalized it away. I have a whole catalog of instances where I ignored my gut reaction and the outcome was not positive. I remember a really critical hiring decision that I was making as a manager, when I hired someone who had a great background, was really charming, and seemed like a good personality fit. Yet, for a reason I could not explain, during the interview I had an intuitive reaction that she wasn't the right person. I quickly rationalized it away, using my Human Resources brain to tell myself I had no real reason on paper not to hire her, so she was hired. She turned out to be exactly as I suspected: briefly charming and then a total disaster. Hey universe, I will not need to learn that lesson again. Just saying.

How to Show Up for Assignments

So, how do you show up for your assignments? You have to first have awareness that there is an assignment before you and a lesson to learn. Once you are aware, you have to be willing to listen and learn (many introverts naturally have this skill). This often means less doing and talking (some go-getter extroverts may be less natural at this).

First, listen and identify if you have seen this lesson before. Perhaps you have not, because you are a quick learner. Or perhaps this is the third time you worked for a narcissist boss, and you recognize it is time to learn the damn lesson already.

Second, when you feel yourself out of alignment, ask your intuition what the lesson is here to learn. Instead of trying to "figure" it out with your head, try and "feel" it out with your heart. Listen quietly for the true right path to appear as an option.

Finally, if you've tried everything, it is time to let go and try complete trust. Sometimes, we feel like we are working so hard and trying everything possible to accomplish something! We might say to ourselves, "It shouldn't be this hard, and why is nothing working?" Perhaps letting go is the one thing you haven't tried. When I have experienced this in my own life, once I released control and truly and freely gave complete trust that the universe had me covered, the universe came through. No explanation. It's just worth a try.

Try It: Assignments and Intuition Activity

Think of an example from the past when a lesson presented itself more than once. Write it down, along with the answers to these questions. Why did it show up again? What prevented you from learning the lesson the first time? What did you do to finally complete the assignment?

Now, think of something that is currently leaving you feeling conflicted. Ask yourself, have you seen this lesson before? What is really bugging you about this situation? Sit and listen to your gut, and ask yourself, what is the next true, right move to complete the assignment and align to your values? Sleep on it before you make a decision, to allow your intuition time to process.

ACTIVITY 8: ALLOWING YOURSELF PERMISSION

"Stop asking people for directions to places
they've never been." – Glennon Doyle

I have always been a rule follower. I like knowing the rules of engagement and living in structure rather than chaos, and I appreciate when things are fair and predictable. When I realized that some of the rules people set for me, or that I set for myself, were not helpful, I saw the opportunity to make new rules for myself. I loved order, but when was it beyond necessary? And exactly whose permission was I waiting for?

Permission from Others

We have grown up our whole lives believing that there is someone else who is granting permission out there, and that we should make sure we have it before we proceed. This came in the form of parents, teachers, coaches, and then bosses approving of our actions. I am not suggesting that these societal structures should be ignored. But we became so used to the muscle memory of always seeking approval from others, that we missed the opportunities to make our own conscious decisions out of pure habit. We seek permission from others in a lot of forms: approval of how we dress and the lifestyle we choose or support from a close family member to go start our own business.

Sometimes, we don't even give others the opportunity to weigh in to give permission, ultimately holding ourselves back. We assume others will not give it, and so we don't ask in the first place. I see this a lot with younger people in their twenties (and I experienced it myself), where we don't ask for something we want because of a high fear of rejection or an assumption that they'll deny it. I remember having a conversation with someone who worked in a relatively flexible job, who would not ask her boss permission to attend a professional development event that would have her getting into the office late at 9:30 a.m. I did the same thing when I was younger, and I wished that my former self (and this young woman) knew that it was totally okay to ask for what she wanted.

What I also know now, is that this was just an example of not giving permission to ourselves.

Permission from Ourselves

The permission we give ourselves is the most powerful type of permission, both when it is granted or withheld.

We give or withhold permission from ourselves, or perhaps, just as importantly, aren't aware enough to ask ourselves before our subconscious shoots us down. We often attach shame to permission, and we tell ourselves we can't have or do something because we don't deserve it. We tell ourselves we shouldn't be happy during a dark time, or we didn't work hard enough to earn it. Think of a time when you whispered that to yourself deep down. Would you ever say that to a friend you cared about? Of course not. But there we are, beating ourselves up and whispering, because we know we aren't supposed to be talking shit to ourselves in the first place.

I find that while both men and women experience this, there is a unique quality in many women that leads us into this trap more frequently. Maybe it is because society has systemically told us to be quiet and take up as little space as possible our whole lives. We subconsciously have heard the message to wait our turn, wait for permission, and someone will let us know when we can go. We can also be masters at accepting the weight of the world on our shoulders, assuming that we can, and should, do it on our own. For men or women alike, there are certainly unconscious stories that we tell ourselves that keep us from embracing the grace and permission to live with joy and freedom.

Here is a new truth to consider: everything is a choice. Sometimes those choices may seem impossible, but they are, in fact, choices. You can become aware of and choose as much happiness as you are willing to authorize for yourself.

Here is a starter list of things to give yourself permission to do:

- Do nothing.

- Have patience.

- Live your dream.

- Release shame and guilt.

- Forgive your or others' missteps.

- Show yourself and others your authentic self.

- Be happy after loss.

- Write new rules for yourself and release the old ones.

- Give yourself the grace that you afford your most treasured friends.

- Start fresh.

For me, I needed to allow myself the permission to be different from the person I always thought I was. I needed to give myself the okay to live without fear of "what if." If I labeled these differently in socially accepted labels, I would say that I have always been an "overachiever" and a "Type A personality," or a good organizer. Those sound like something to really aspire to, right? And therein lies the problem. We want ourselves and our kids to be successful, well-adjusted, organized, bound for big things. But if we only show that we want more and more of these behaviors and we never say that it is enough, it can be hard for high-achievers to know when to stop. And those words that sound so good as descriptions are just tinder for some really outrageous internal dialogues.

One of my biggest problems was how closely I identified with being a high-achiever. If I'm not a high-achiever, does that mean that I must be a low-achiever? If I'm not organized, does that mean I have to walk around like Flighty Hot Mess Barbie? I always saw the alternative options as binary, black or white. The other side of the coin didn't look very inviting in that light. There had to be a "Door Number Three" to a world where I didn't have to be either a psycho or a degenerate.

I had to allow myself the idea that I could achieve big things, without carrying the heavy weight of feeling like it could all fall apart at any moment if I took my foot off the gas. This was the fear of "what if." What if I failed a test? What if I got fired from a job? I know now that those lessons would have been valuable in the end result, but in my old state before recognizing the opportunity to change, I would have been sure that those failures would have ruined my empire, as if my whole life up until that point was weighing on the outcome of that one test or that one job. Now, I allow myself the permission to take the good (e.g., the motivation) and shed the parts that are weighing me down (e.g., the fear).

In her book, *Braving the Wilderness*, Brené Brown describes a practice that she uses for giving herself permission. Over the years, she has written herself countless permission slips. Just like the ones that you sign for your children to attend a field trip at school, you take a piece of paper and explicitly write out the permission you are granting for yourself. In the book, she describes how she wrote herself a permission slip to have fun while filming Super Soul Sunday with Oprah. And so, she did. Brené also reminds us that having permission is part of the equation, but walking forward and doing it is another part of it.

One way to really solidify change and hold yourself accountable is to tell someone about what you are doing and the new permission you are allowing for yourself. Tell your coach, a trusted friend, or anyone else who can be supportive and hold space for you to do your work. If others ask you about it and call you out when you are not honoring your new rule, you will feel more inclined to hold yourself to it.

Try It: Permission Activity

Here is an activity that you can use to pinpoint where you can allow yourself permission.

- Find just one thing you are not giving yourself permission for. What is it? Write it down.
- Write down the current statement you are telling yourself about that topic, the sentence that sums up why you are blocking your own permission and peace for that area of your life.
- Write down a new rule that allows you the permission you are seeking from yourself. This should be a kinder, more supportive, and expansive version that allows you all the possibility you need. Put it on notes in prominent places to get used to the new idea.
- Take one small, first action toward doing what you want to do and living this new possibility. Extra credit, over-achiever? Take another step. And another. And another.

ACTIVITY 9: EXPERIMENTS IN BOLD MOVES

"Sometimes I've believed as many as six impossible things before breakfast." – Lewis Carroll

Just the other day, three people over the course of 24 hours called me courageous. To be honest, this was never really a word that I associated myself with for most of my life.

As an introvert, I am not someone who has regularly spoken up loudly or talked in a meeting just to talk. I speak when I have something to say, and the rest of the time I spend listening and observing. As you can imagine, when people don't witness outward acts of courage, persistence, or blabbering, sometimes they make assumptions that you aren't very daring. Without a doubt, I have missed opportunities to be courageous in my life and career, but I also refuse to subscribe to this one-dimensional description of what courage should look like.

I heard this story a lot early in my career. I worked for a company that had a strong culture and regularly used leadership competencies as a common language to describe people's strengths and weaknesses, and to help leaders frame up their personal feedback for their teams. I regularly received feedback that I needed to demonstrate more courage. I heard this enough that it still comes as a surprise when someone tells me directly that they think I am courageous. At the same time, I know that is an old story about my leadership that just simply isn't true anymore, and it wasn't the whole truth then either.

One of the key actions I practiced while going through my recent period of transformation described in this book was to experiment in bold moves. I was feeling stuck, and I wanted to purposely and regularly put myself out of my comfort zone to stretch the limits. I looked for ways, big and small, to go outside what I would normally do, by either doing something totally different or by stretching what I was doing to be much bigger. And I worked to eliminate the people and situations that made me feel small.

I began to realize part of the equation with taking bold moves meant taking risks. If I look back at my history, it is quite clear that I have, in fact, never taken on a risk that I couldn't master. It appears that I have accomplished a lot in my life and career, and I have. But what I had never done was to put myself in a situation where I could possibly fail when it was really important. Here is the pattern: I did everything well, but was never particularly great at anything. I swam on the varsity swim team, but I was never the best. I danced in the best competitive dance group, but I was never the best dancer. I went to a good college, but not a university where I was out of my league. What if I had applied for an Ivy League school? What if I got accepted? That would have been scary as hell, because I would have felt a little out over my skis. Nope. A quality business program at a state school is totally something I could nail. I had a proven track record of playing it safe and being among the best in an environment that was never going to get the better of me.

When I made the commitment to begin experimenting in bold moves, I realized I needed to take risks, but I also needed to start small to build up my danger tolerance over time. For me, the answer was not to go out, buy a motorcycle, take up base jumping, or take other completely uncalculated risks. It was about following my heart and stretching the dream and the action to be bigger than it ever was before.

Here are some of the ways I purposely exercised my courage muscles, to give you some ideas:

Find tiny, everyday ways to step out of your rut. I read articles from totally new sources to learn how other perspectives (ones I didn't even know existed) were formed. When I went to restaurants I knew well, I ordered something abnormal off the menu that I would have normally ignored. I rode a bike for the first time in over 15 years (I had a few falls in my youth and never really got back on my bike after that, until now). I would drive down roads I had never been on, just to finally find out what was there. Having this "every moment" mentality of trying new things and being uncomfortable helped grow resiliency for some of the bigger exercises.

Surround yourself with next level people. I actively sought to meet people and build relationships with people who were inspiring and made me want to rise to their level. I approached it with a beginner's mindset and wanted to constantly feel as if I had much to learn. I could only hope to give value back to the community of badassery that I was curating. Over a year later, I am amazed at the collective brilliance of the people who surround me. It makes me better and always keeps me on my toes.

Put yourself in uncomfortable situations. Warning: this does not mean unsafe situations or dark alley lurking. To give myself a regular few moments of heart-pounding each week, I joined an impromptu public speaking group. Since (like many introverts) I much prefer to be very prepared before I speak, impromptu freaks me out. I spent time with people I would have never met at events I would have never experienced if I hadn't made a conscious choice to be completely out of my element. It has been exhilarating and easy to see the progress of gaining comfort and courage in what was previously untouchable.

Dream bigger – to the true end game. While I still fall back into "planning small" versus "dreaming big" now and again, I constantly ask myself if the goal I am considering could be bigger, and then I put the universe in motion to help handle it. I frequently ask my clients what they want in life and then challenge them to dream bigger. Their answers go from getting that promotion this year (planning small) to President of the organization (dreaming big), a dream they probably never actually even said out loud before. Once you stop stunting yourself with too-small goals, then write down the big end game, make a good old-fashioned vision board, write a one-year and five-year vision to put in exact detail what that looks like, and stay out of your own way.

Act as if it were already happening. Once I decided on my big, hairy goal, I acted as if it was already happening. I decided in 2017 that I was finally going to go after my bucket list item of doing a TEDx talk. I began with a mindset of desperation, hoping I would get accepted, and then felt devastated when I saw the rejection note and thought, "I'll never get selected." Instead, I applied at another city and wrote a new (and much improved) topic, and already knew the next three cities where I would apply if I didn't get accepted. My new approach was to act as if it was already happening. It was no longer a matter of IF I would do a TEDx talk, it was a matter of WHEN. I took a class on how to construct and give a good talk, before I was ever accepted as a speaker anywhere. I had my whole talk written before I applied. And, the very next one I applied for, I was selected. My bucket list turned from stuff I want to do someday far away to things I am going to accomplish this year.

Bucket list, you just got leveled up.

Try It: Bold Moves Activity

Pick something scary. I will let you decide if you have to start small here or if you have the chops to go big, but don't sell yourself short. The key is to create the feelings of discomfort, then exhilaration, and perhaps pride. Do you have your hairy scary in mind? Good. Write it down.

Now write down a bigger version of that goal. And write a bigger version of that bigger goal. And finally, write an even bigger version. Where did you end up? Pick the biggest one you are willing to take on. If it doesn't feel scary, you aren't focused on the right thing or the right scope. Go bigger.

Write down the very next step that you are going to take toward that goal (just the one next step). Add in when you are going to do it by and how you will know you've completed it. Then, go do it, and journal about how it felt to stretch.

Rinse and repeat.

ACTIVITY 10: BE STILL AND ALONE

"Love works miracles in stillness." – Herbert Read

I do my best work alone. Of course, I have to interact and collaborate with other people constantly, and this is critical for me to be able to do great work later. However, I need time and space to myself to really be able to dial into my best ideas, which is a classic introvert tendency. How I ever got any work done at all in a corporate or operational setting where I was usually too busy to eat or pee is beyond me. As I reflect now, even though I always did great work, I was nowhere near maximizing my potential, because I did not have enough space or time to process and create.

This is often the undiagnosed problem for high-achieving introverts; our work is always successful, so we are completely unaware of even bigger levels of greatness that we could be reaching. We just stop because it is excellent, or we keep doing what we are doing because it appears to be working. We don't even realize on a conscious level that we could be doing bigger or better work, but deep down on a subconscious level we know because we feel busy yet unfulfilled.

It is important as well that we make the distinction between more work and better work. Often, high-achievers get more responsibility added to their plates because they will make it happen, or it is "good for their career." Doing more work that isn't stretching you or expanding your repertoire in some way is simply more of the same, not bigger or better. We confuse this a lot in the corporate world with "development," but in the case of a high-achieving introvert, it is simply choking the blank space and time needed for introverts to do their best work. I remember feeling at odds with my personal values of only doing work with excellence, because there was so much to be done. Eventually, "done is better than perfect" became an overused rationalization. I would get worn down enough to not even care about or celebrate completion, because I was just glad it was finally done. But what if it could be so much better?

Regardless of your current work environment, having the awareness that you need time and space in solitude for your own thoughts to thrive, is the first part of what you need to start building your life to include those things regularly. Like anything, it is a habit-building process that takes some time and effort, but here are some methods you can try that will begin to hold the space that you need.

Build the Time You Require into Your Schedule

Are you someone who thrives on back-to-back meetings, or do you prefer space in between to gather your thoughts? I often had back-to-back meetings and celebrated my ninja-like efficiency, but in reality, I needed time in between to decompress from the last conversation and gather my thoughts for the next one. I also HATE being late, and so that buffer time in between meetings was critical for me to get to my destination early enough so as not to get stressed about time. I could also use my early extra minutes to look over my notes and get centered on the next topic. If building in time in-between meetings just simply isn't possible (and I challenge you that if you want it bad enough, it is possible), then you can hold a large preparation time earlier where you organize all of your thoughts, put your topics in an organized fashion in your likely color-coded folders, and whisk on to your action-packed day.

I know you know how to be organized. You probably have lots of fancy tabs and folders in your desk that bring you joy. It is likely you are not honoring the time you need to do your next level work, because you are rationalizing it away and giving it to something less important. Email is a great example of a time suck that does nothing to add to your good work or bring you joy. If you spend the only quiet, longer blocks of alone time that you have answering other peoples' emails, then you are squandering your best potential moments.

I know my brain has a lot of complex thoughts that are sometimes difficult to form into coherent and articulate sentences, particularly on the fly. Humans only have so much RAM in their brain for working on multiple things at the same time, and introverts with big ideas can use up maximum capacity. And then there is the utter annoyance I feel when my deep thought processes are interrupted. It often takes a minute for me to resurface from where I was, and by the time I finish with someone else's question, I have lost my place in my internal think tank, or have lost a lot of time in transit to and from my heavy thinking.

If you need 30 minutes between meetings, build it on your calendar. If you need gym or coffee shop time on the way home to relax, then plan it out as a recurring appointment. If you need time to center, meditate, or set intentions, make it a morning ritual before anyone else in the house is awake. The awareness and commitment to giving yourself time and space might be the missing link to unlocking even higher potential.

When I left the corporate environment, I retooled my schedule to be exactly to my ideal. It balanced time with others and time alone. It included exercise, time out in nature, blank space for "curiosity hour" to Google topics I wanted to learn about, and uninterrupted blocks for actual work. If I could do a high-powered job, the actual work I had to do, in about 6 hours a week in between useless conference calls and soul-sucking meetings, then doing my actual work in 20 hours a week seemed like a total gift. The other 20 hours became dedicated to all of the other stuff that made my life worth living and informed my work, like reading. I recognize that not everyone has the opportunity to completely own their schedule, but deciding what your priorities are, scheduling them first, and holding onto that time like grim death is a surefire way to start. If you aren't sure what your priorities are, go back to the top and read the Values section.

Meditate

I have struggled for years with keeping a consistent meditation practice, because I tended to view it in very black and white terms. I thought I needed to meditate a long time and be really focused or just not do it at all. In reality, I have found (and research confirms) that even a few minutes a day of mindfulness or meditation can have a lasting impact on your day. The whole point is to quiet your mind, not to have it quiet already when you begin! I come out the other side feeling calm and focused, which makes my scheduled thinking and creative time much more productive.

Introverts often have a very rich inner dialogue going on in their heads at all times (you've already met the Board of Directors), and on top of that, many of us have big jobs, kids at home, parents to care for, and a thousand other things that we are trying to hold in our working memory at any given time. I generally have a very ambitious multi-tasker brain that I am sure if you photographed would look like about 1,200 monkeys swinging around in a small patch of jungle. In fact, I can feel myself being distant and distracted when I am trying to hold too many things in my head at the same time. Much like a computer, our brains can only hold and process so much.

Meditating allows you to cut through that and be more focused on the few key important things. Much like scheduling time for your thoughts, this can be a good start to those longer blocks of scheduled time to stay focused rather than frittering your "introvert spa time" away on emails.

Intentions

During your meditation time or at the start of your quiet work hour, take time to think and to set an intention for the day. This may reflect the biggest and most important work you do that day, or it may reflect just being or living with joy. Taking a moment to set an intention will be a moment of consciously setting a path for the day. When things veer off course, you will be aware that you are not living your intention and you can redirect. If you didn't set one to begin with, you will never take action to get back on a course you never set.

If you don't know where you're going, any road will take you there. - Lewis Carroll
Have you ever had one of those days where you leave work and you can't remember a single important thing that you did that day? You just spent ten hours at work, bouncing from one thing to the next and you can't think of one thing to talk about at the dinner table when asked how your day was. Those are the days I wish I could go back to. I would set an intention, be more focused throughout the day, and come out the other side feeling like it wasn't a total waste. It was days like this that, particularly as a new parent, I would think, "I left my beautiful baby at daycare for a day full of this? I'd rather be at home cleaning shit and getting puked on than wasting the day for nothing." Intentions might have helped.

My intention that I set for the day tends to align with my top three priorities, and simply writing those down on paper suddenly takes power away from the menial junk that fills my day. I find myself doing less of anything that doesn't honor my intention, or Top Three, for the day. If my day fills up with other "stuff," then I reflect at the end of the day what went well and what I could improve the next day. As a result, I have much fewer days that waste away, and the ones that do get a post-mortem for improvement tomorrow.

Gratitude and Journaling

I have incorporated a gratitude practice in my day in order to expand the good things in my life. Sometimes it has been focused on a specific topic, and other times it has been free-form. I write them down in a journal next to my bed at the start of the day, at the end of the day, or as part of my daily journal and to-do list at my desk. Find what method works for you. You will begin to see things that you didn't previously notice.

If you express gratitude once, you cover the obvious bases. Family, friends, health, and so on. But if you do it daily, you can't use the same tired list every day, so instead of just saying "family," you begin to note your gratitude for the time when you call your mom every Monday, or when your child comes home having learned a new song at school that is so cute to listen to. Instead of "friends," you notice your gratitude for your friend who always texts to check in on you, or that you had the opportunity to send a meal over to new parents. You become grateful for the fact that you haven't had a cold in three months or that your routine doctor appointment was, in fact, just routine. It gets more granular, and as a result, your gratitude expands.

Just like your intentions, writing your gratitude down gives you the personal accountability to make sure you commit to it on paper, and it sends it out into the universe. It is easy to recite gratitude in your head without actually thinking of new topics, but when you write it down, it forces you to be much more committed and deliberate with the practice. And, it is fascinating to read back what you wrote months ago as a study on how you have changed in the meantime. To take it to even the next level, express your gratitude to others for the things that you write down. Maybe you tell that friend how much it means to you that they check in with you often, and why. They will feel honored by your gratitude and will probably keep up the good work.

Thinking List & Curiosity Hour

In order to clear out working memory in my brain for things that are really important, I like to make different lists to capture my thoughts and go back to them at a later time when I have my designated quiet time to reflect. I keep separate lists based on what the action might be, so that my most important "To Do" list doesn't get muddied by things I wanted to look into, or people I wanted to reach out to when I got around to it. These are all separate lists. When I want to get shit done, I go to the To Do list. When I want to reach out to my network community, I go to that list and focus on connecting. When I want to research new ideas or topics that sparked my interest, I go to the Curiosity Hour list.

Curiosity Hour is my favorite. A friend gave me this practice, and it has both cleaned up my To Do list and created this lovely running list of cool things I want to research. Sometimes I Google a topic, read up on one page, and that is sufficient before moving on to the next topic. Sometimes I research down a rabbit hole if it is something I really want to learn more about. It's a great way to allow your mind to learn and wander with purpose.

If you do not plan time on your calendar for this type of blank space, I guarantee you will never do it. That is not to say you don't waste time "researching," but you are probably just doing it more in an "hour lost on Instagram" sort of way (no judging, it happens to the best of us). Especially for people like myself who need time to decompress alone, we find ways to do it one way or the other because we need it to recharge. If you are intentional about your time, you can spend it in a more fulfilling way for your personal development than wasting it doing something you aren't really even enjoying. I troll around Facebook when I have no chance of doing anything else productive, like at 9:00 p.m.

Creative Time

It has become increasingly clear to me as I spend my "blank space" time more effectively, that holding space for creative work is critical to my wellbeing. Growing up, I was most in flow when I was doing something creative. I spent a lot of time singing, dancing, and acting, and those were the moments when I was most perfectly myself and enjoying life. It felt easy and free. So why as an adult was I not spending any time in a creative space?

Once I got over myself and realized what a good time that was, I decided to spend more of my time there and see what happened. I spent more time singing and dancing, listening to more music, and lo and behold, trying a new creative outlet that had always been dying to escape from my introvert body: writing. Imagine that! Spend time researching, thinking, reflecting, and writing ideas quietly in my office to create something uniquely. my own? Sign me up. Perhaps your creative time is best spent on graphic design, or crafting, or coding. This is just another way to commit to the personal time that you need, and to use it in a way that makes you feel so alive that you keep doing it and refuse to give it up for anyone else.

I have covered a lot of different ways to be still and commit to some time alone, but they all hinge on the idea that you give yourself the time you need. If you are skeptical, try it for a period of time (I suggest 30 days), and, in the grand scheme of things, it is easy to go back wasting your time on email and Facebook without much lost if you don't like it after that time. But if you do like it, you will have unlocked additional time in your day and week, because you spent it with intention and purpose rather than fitting in some "skim milk" version of "you time" in between useless meetings.

I could not successfully do all of the other work of living out my new action plan if I didn't have these practices in place to allow myself time and space to be still and be alone. As an introvert, I needed that time to process all of the new information that I had taken in with the deliberate practice and growth that I was experiencing. Had I not allowed myself this space and protected it,

I would have been a mess. It would have been as if I hadn't slept and allowed my brain to dream and process memories overnight. And if you have ever been truly deprived of sleep, you know that is a dark place to avoid. So why wouldn't you allow yourself the same courtesy during the day? It allows the high-achiever in us to accomplish big things without the weight and judgement of how we "should" be spending our time.

Try It: Still and Alone Activity

Commit to yourself an amount of time each day that you will spend being still and alone. Maybe it is an hour. Perhaps you think mustering up 10 minutes is going to be a challenge. Whatever it is, you decide. You have to be all in.

Consider when exactly you will schedule this time so that it works with your day and no one will steal it from you. Put it on the schedule every day for seven days. This is an experiment, so you want to try it on work days and non-work days to see what works for you. Add it in your calendar with notifications.

Start your time with a minimum of one minute of breathing and centering. You spend the rest of the time however you want. Perhaps you spend your full allotted 10 minutes on meditating, or maybe you breathe and center for two minutes before you spend the next 25 minutes reading or writing quietly. After one week, assess what worked, what adjustments to make, and block it in your calendar with no end date ever!

ACTIVITY 11: STAYING FRIENDS WITH YOUR INNER CHILD

"The most sophisticated people I know – inside they're all children. We never really lose a certain sense we had when we were kids." – Jim Henson

I have often felt as an adult that I am really just an eight-year-old trapped in an adult's body. I like music, jokes, board games, cartoons, and hiding tiny animal figurines in peoples' purses. In my best state, I was someone who saw the world with wonderment and joy, much like a child. I swear to you, Santa might be real.

An old friend showed me some photographs recently from our epic middle school sleepovers and birthday parties. Every photo showed me hanging upside down with a giant cheesy grin on my face or making weird faces at the camera. It was the perfect representation of me as a child before I changed anything to suit anyone else's interests, particularly Bridget's. It occurred to me while I was on this journey that, somewhere along the way, I had forgotten about my inner child. I had stuffed her away and asked her to please grow up, and I took on my new role as the fun police. When I tried to identify the last time I really felt in the flow, I had to think back. Way back. The fact that I didn't have a very recent example of sustained flow and enjoyment was a red flag.

The times that I felt most in the flow of life were when I was doing the things I loved most as a child: swimming laps for the swim team, dancing at dance practice, singing in the choir, or joining a theater show. It was pure fun without expectation or pressure. As I grew older, the weight grew, too, but in their purest forms, my childhood activities were havens of joy and alignment.

It struck me that I didn't have any outlets like this in my life anymore as a thirty-something working mom, so I set out to revisit my old stomping grounds to see if they still had any magic left in them. I switched up my morning running workout and went to the outdoor pool. It was cold and reminiscent. I dusted off my tap shoes and went to a tap class. Although my feet forgot a few steps, the hour flew by. I took a midday break to go watch a musical at the local theater and sang the entire soundtrack of *Wicked* at the top of my lungs in the shower. I pulled out the piano sheet music. I listened to French music and felt nostalgia from my time studying abroad.

I like kids (and adult kids) because there is just the purest zest for life about them. If you are ever unsure, watch a bunch of children when a bubble machine starts up or go see a cartoon movie on a Saturday matinee. It is pure, unbridled joy. I want to live that way, too!

Since I have worked hard to let go of fear, ditch work that isn't a "hell yes," and allow myself the permission to live an awesome life, the one thing missing was adding back in the things that bring me joy. I certainly love much of the way I spend my personal time now as an adult. I value that I have taken up running and that I have a three-year-old who reminds me to play every day. These are whole new sources of joy for me. But a little tap dancing now and then wouldn't hurt.

I have found that when I am stressed or feeling immense pressure, there is no room in my brain for anything extra, and that means all of the fun gets cataloged in the back. I become quick-tempered, distracted, and boring. When I allow myself the space to release the pressure, suddenly my brain has extra capacity to no longer rush to the next thing but to savor the moment. I read an extra book to my son before bedtime, am more available for hugs, and look for ways to fill time with joy.

The lesson learned is to stay friends with your inner child. Go back and identify the things that brought you joy or allowed you to be in the flow in your younger years before you adulted them to death. See how you can recreate or revisit those feelings of fun and flow, and how those can then, in turn, inform the rest of your work and life. Creative time is not wasted time, and having time for enjoyment is not irresponsible (I have learned). It actually feeds energy into the rest of our lives.

If we think only of managing our lives by managing time, it is a zero-sum game that never seems to add up. We are always trying to fit ten pounds in a five-pound bag. But if we look instead at managing our energy, energy can be limitless, and instead of time always passing, energy can be gained or lost depending on how we spend time. You could spend one hour of time checking more email (joy suck) or you could spend that same hour at a dance class (energy feeder). If you manage your energy instead of time, then you will make sure that you have activities that fuel your soul and give you energy to be able to fund the other parts of your day that require an energy expenditure. I found that staying friends with my inner child was just what I needed to stay grounded in joy and manage my energy more effectively.

Try It: Inner Child Activity

Think back to a time when you were younger and you were totally in the flow of what you were doing. Hours could pass when you were doing this without you noticing, and you were in a place of total enjoyment without concern for what the rest of the world was doing or thinking. You were "dancing like nobody's watching," so to speak.

Pick one or two things that come to mind for you, and go do them. Get excited before you go, by quietly reflecting on how you felt in that younger time and how you want to feel today. Put a name to that feeling. Go do it, and have fun! Find that mental place where you don't worry about anyone else in the moment.

Afterward, reflect on how it felt. Did it bring you energy? If so, go again, and if not, understand why not. Keep searching until you can find joy and your inner child in a way that feeds your energy bank.

ACTIVITY 12: THE ACTION PLAN

"Every day of our lives we are on the verge of making those slight changes that would make all the difference." – Mignon McLaughlin

Toward the end of my existential crisis, I realized I was ready to move forward. After taking in the newfound awareness about myself both past and present, I had to pause for a minute to map out my next moves. This was a place I had never been before, and I was headed toward uncharted territory. It was time for an action plan.

This could be no ordinary action plan. It wasn't the time to set goals that I was firmly sure I could achieve, or to set SMART objectives that followed a plan. It was the moment to do this differently and to break the cycle of attachment to the outcome. The action plan had to be all about the journey rather than the end goal. This would mean truly focusing on changing behavior, and the importance would be in making hundreds of tiny moves and decisions to build some new muscles, rather than one big goal or event to work toward. I could already tell this was out of my comfort zone.

From the Lemon Pancake Monologue (my existential crisis conversation in Chapter 9), here were the specific steps I had chosen to start making a change in my life.

What specific steps could I take to unburden myself from these intense pressures when I feel or experience them?

1. Recognize them, say, that's interesting, and then study it like a scientist who is not attached to the outcome of the experiment (judgement free).

2. Practice a higher "hell yes" threshold.

3. Build out my manifesto – what I stand for privately and publicly.

4. Experiments in bold moves (living with purpose, being larger, overcoming fear).

5. These felt like small changes for big problems. Could this possibly be all that it took? The answer was yes.

Study It Like a Scientist

Let's say that you were invited to watch a psychology experiment at the local university, and you had the chance to sit behind the two-way mirror room to watch the human subjects act all human with a bucket of popcorn and enjoy the show. Would you do it? You better believe it! That's better than television.

Now, let's say you were the subject of the study, and you had the opportunity to watch the behavior unfold as if it were an out-of-body experience, but you made no judgements, good or bad, about what you were doing. You were just there to examine and dictate notes on your observations, like, "Hmmmm, that is interesting. Subject appears to show angst with an increase in blood pressure when she makes large-scale goals for herself."

That is how you study it like a scientist. If you can detach yourself from the outcome of the experiment, you can be open-minded to what you see and how things turn out. Quality experiments are not set up so they get the conclusion they think they should, but rather to confirm or discredit a hypothesis. In my case, I would first recognize a negative physical reaction, or how I was feeling. I would then say to myself, "Hmmm, that is interesting," and try to determine from a neutral position what caused that negative reaction. I could trace back my feelings to the stress or intense pressures I was putting on myself. By not adding additional judgement to the pressure I was already feeling, I kept the problem from getting so big that it was unmanageable. Breaking the cycle of self-judgement allowed me to think rationally, about consciously choosing a different thought that did not apply pressure to myself.

Practice a Higher "Hell Yes" Threshold

Sometimes I can feel overwhelmed by the growing "To Do" list of stuff that needs to be done. The first step to releasing this pressure is to just start taking things off the list. Less stuff, fewer shoulds, less pressure. Now, this is not a quick and easy fix when it is something you have attached your worth to for a long time. I have always been a list maker and a list slayer, but never a list minimizer. I began going down the list, line by line, asking myself these questions:

- Is this important/urgent? (And if so, who says it is? Is it REALLY?)

- Is this a "hell yes?"

- Is this a necessary insurance policy?

First, if it doesn't fit into the important or urgent buckets, it just goes away. I also check myself on who thinks it is urgent or important, and if that is really true. I even ferreted out a few things that were posing as important because Bridget, the inner critic, thought they were. In her new job assignment, she is not authorized to make those decisions.

Second, it either needed to be deemed a "hell yes" or a necessary insurance policy to proceed. A "hell yes" are those things that you are genuinely excited for, that you don't put off and that set your soul on fire. They are the reason you bother doing anything. They are also the things where you are playing bigger, living your purpose, and checking things off the bucket list. These are not hard to identify. I once listed out some goals and planning for the next six months, and my own coach said to me, "Katie, I am pretty sure you didn't leave your corporate job to quote, 'find a graphic designer.'" Damn it, she was right. Finding a graphic designer was a task, but not a goal that brought my passions alive.

While doing only "hell yes" things sounds glorious, I also recognized that my life and my business could not run on love alone, so there is some work that is necessary and doesn't spark joy in me. These are all of the things that I have determined that I do really need to do, even if they don't excite me, because they *enable* the "hell yes" list. But if I compartmentalize them here in the "insurance" list, they don't creep into my "hell yes" list and act as if that is all I have time to complete. This keeps me out of the trap of pushing paper around all day, never accomplishing anything big or scary or great. I make sure that I reserve time on my calendar that reflects both "hell yes" and "insurance" work, as well as all of the other time I mentioned earlier in the book, like exercising and Curiosity Hour.

Build Out My Manifesto

There are a few ways to look at this that might sound familiar to you: find your why (Simon Sinek-style), write your personal mission statement, or define your truth. Because it can be so easy to pile on things that don't matter or don't contribute to the overarching goal, it was critical for me to understand exactly what I was doing, why I was doing it, and measure everything against that. If I couldn't justify something in my life as part of my own manifesto, then why the hell was I doing it? Enough already.

I have done versions of all of these different methods to the same end, where it boils down to *why you do what you do*. But my idea behind building out my manifesto was bigger than that. It was the opposite of distilling my purpose down to one word or phrase; it was getting clear on where I stood across a lot of different opinions and areas of my life. Without a clear opinion on something, I often did nothing in response. By building out my manifesto and consciously deciding what I stood for in my life and work, I could do more to act accordingly, fight for what I believed in, or recognize when I was going against my beliefs.

I thought about, decided on, and solidified my belief system as the foundation for taking action. This meant assuming I know the answer, not waiting for someone else to provide it. This meant deciding my stance on political or social issues and speaking about them (while reserving the right to change). This meant no longer putting myself in situations where I was going against the grain of my values and what I stood for. This meant being vulnerable and having an opinion even when it wasn't popular.

This was all in the name of getting off the fence. I could no longer sit in the neutral zone, living with inaction. Building out what I stood for personally and professionally (and let's be honest, that is all of the same thing) was a critical step in taking more action, and acted as a personal compass as I navigated the uncharted waters of releasing self-inflicted pressure and expectations, and putting an end to attaching my value to achievement. Here is how that began to look differently:

- Instead of looking for a non-profit board to be a part of, I removed myself from committees and leadership roles. I took on one new thing: being a coach for one underprivileged girl.

- I did less "networking" and instead spent that time having conversations on how to change education, economics, or housing for poor areas of my city.

- I began spending my time with purpose, rather than achievement, in mind. It was freeing, and living in my newfound definition of success felt real.

Experiments in Bold Moves

This was so big that I spent a whole chapter already to cover it. By far, this required the most ongoing maintenance, and resulted in some serious growth and flexing of resiliency muscles over the course of months. This was the emotional equivalent to doing hundreds of sprints over time as a training regimen. The bold moves made my heart pound and my palms sweat, but the deliberate practice, at first uncomfortable, became easier over time. Pushing myself to think bigger and act as if those things were already happening, led me further than I could have imagined. It pushed dreams and ideas into reality.

The old version of me would have been crushed by an edifice of judgment and self-inflicted pressure and the weight of my rising expectations. It would have felt unbearable and impossible. Because I lit a flame thrower to my old way of thinking, I could find new ways to make my big dreams and ideas a reality, but without the weight (most of the time, nobody's perfect). This is being a high-achiever without the weight, and it is, in fact, easy, free, and without walls or boundaries.

Try It: Action Plan Activity

Wait and do this until you find a day when you feel inclined to slash and burn your To Do List, and make some bold decisions. Take a look at your calendar bookings and your To Do list. Go through with a very discerning eye and decide if it is a "hell yes," a critical "insurance" item that enables the "hell yes" list, or it is something that can just go away. Clean house, y'all. If you find you don't have any "hell yes" items, it is time to put your dreaming hat on and write on paper the things you want to do but have been too scared to admit to yourself, until now.

Look at your calendar, you're going to need to make room for all of this cool stuff you want to do. Get rid of stuff that pertained to the list you crossed off and things other people think you "should" do that don't match with your goals, your "hell yes" list, or your insurance. Plan the time in to your week that you need. If you have to prioritize and not do everything all at once, that is normal and human. If you try and do everything all at once, that is your shit-talking inner critic acting as your secretary.

Repeat this as often as you have to. It might be as often as weekly, perhaps quarterly. Regular maintenance is key and will reinvigorate you on how excited you are to accomplish the "hell yes" list.

THE ENDING
(OR, COMMENCEMENT)

"Don't be willing to accept an ordinary life."
– Salle Merrill Bedfield

I share these stories and tools with you with one purpose: to share and feel love and understanding. That is the why behind all of my work. I believe that if we all felt loved, understood, and a sense of belonging, then the world would be the exact place that we are hoping to make it. Hell, if 10% of us got there, that would be a critical tipping point. It makes the work worth doing.

The minute we are no longer willing to accept and tolerate the things in our life that are holding us back from our true greatness, we can start to see the path forward into living a life in technicolor. When I imagine myself on my deathbed, I can see fireworks and bright colors, and my heart bursting with meaning, purpose, and love. There is not an email or a conference call in sight.

This is not the end, but the beginning. Your beginning. Make it count.

REFERENCES & RECOMMENDED READING

Chapter 1: The Weight

Rasoul, Katie. *Uncovering the High-Achieving Introvert.* TEDxUWMilwaukee, September 2017. https://www.youtube.com/watch?v=4zV1Y8IShds.

Chapter 2: The High-Achieving Introvert

Aron, Elaine. *The Highly Sensitive Person: How to Thrive When the World Overwhelms You.* New York: Broadway Books, 1997.

Cain, Susan. *Quiet: The Power of Introverts in a World That Can't Stop Talking.* New York: Broadway Books, 2012.

Chandler, Steve and Rich Litvin. *The Prosperous Coach: Increase Income and Impact for You and Your Clients.* Anna Maria, FL: Maurice Bassett, 2013.

Granneman, Jenn. *The Secret Life of Introverts: Inside Our Hidden World*. New York: Skyhorse Publishing, 2017.

Chapter 3: Growing Up

Gendler, J. Ruth. *The Book of Qualities*. New York: HarperPerennial, 1988.

Activity 1: Values and Value

Byron, Katie. *Loving What Is: Four Questions That Can Change Your Life*. New York: Harmony Books, 2002.

Gilbert, Elizabeth. *Your Elusive Creative Genius*. TED Conference 2009. https://www.ted.com/talks/elizabeth_gilbert_on_genius.

Petriglieri, Jennifer and Gianpiero Petriglieri. *The Talent Curse*, Harvard Business Review. From the May-June 2017 Issue. https://hbr.org/2017/05/the-talent-curse.

Activity 2: Definition of Success

Dudley, Drew. *Everyday Leadership*. TEDxToronto, September 2010. https://www.ted.com/talks/drew_dudley_everyday_leadership.

Halvorson, Heidi Grant. *How to Keep Happiness From Fading*. Psychology Today, posted August 15, 2012. https://www.psychologytoday.com/blog/the-science-success/201208/how-keep-happiness-fading.

Sull, Donald and Dominic Houlder. *Do Your Commitments Match Your Convictions?* Havard Business Review, January 2005. https://hbr.org/2005/01/do-your-commitments-match-your-convictions.

Activity 3: What to Do, and What to Give Up

Kondo, Marie. *The Life-Changing Magic of Tidying Up: The Japanese Art of Decluttering and Organizing.* Berkeley, CA: Ten Speed Press, 2014.

McKeown, Greg. *Essentialism: The Disciplined Pursuit of Less.* New York: Crown Business, 2014.

Activity 5: Feeling "Enough"

Brown, Brené. *The Power of Vulnerability.* TEDxHouston, June 2010. https://www.ted.com/talks/brene_brown_on_vulnerability.

Activity 6: Fear of Future

Ferriss, Tim. *Fear-Setting: The Most Valuable Exercise I Do Every Month.* The Tim Ferris Blog, posted May 15, 2017. https://tim.blog/2017/05/15/fear-setting.

Ferriss, Tim. *Why you should define your fears instead of your goals.* TED 2017. https://www.ted.com/talks/tim_ferriss_why_you_should_define_your_fears_instead_of_your_goals.

Robbins, Mel. *The 5 Second Rule: Transform your Life, Work, and Confidence with Everyday Courage.* Savio Republic, 2017.

Sandberg, Sheryl and Adam Grant. *Option B: Facing Adversity, Building Resilience, and Finding Joy.* New York: Alfred A. Knopf, 2017.

Sandberg, Sheryl and Adam Grant. *Sheryl Sandberg and Adam Grant on Resilience.* HBR IdeaCast, posted April 27, 2017. https://hbr.org/ideacast/2017/04/sheryl-sandberg-and-adam-grant-on-resilience.

Schulte, Brigid. *Harvard neuroscientist: Meditation not only reduces stress, here's how it changes your brain.* Washington Post, posted May 26, 2015. https://www.washingtonpost.com/news/inspired-life/wp/2015/05/26/harvard-neuroscientist-meditation-not-only-reduces-stress-it-literally-changes-your-brain.

Activity 7: Showing Up When Your Assignments Come

Bernstein, Gabrielle. *The Universe Has Your Back: Transform Fear to Faith.* Hay House, 2016.

Day, Laura. *Practical Intuition: How to Harness the Power of Your Instinct and Make It Work for You.* New York: Broadway Books, 1996.

Activity 8: Allowing Yourself Permission

Brown, Brené. *Braving the Wilderness: The Quest for True Belonging and the Courage to Stand Alone.* New York: Random House, 2017.

Activity 9: Experiments in Bold Moves

LaPorte, Danielle. *The Fire Starter Sessions: A Soulful and Practical Guide to Creating Success on Your Own Terms.* New York: Harmony Books, 2012.

Strayed, Cheryl. *Wild: From Lost to Found on the Pacific Crest Trail.* New York: Vintage Books, 2013.

Activity 10: Be Still and Alone

Bays, Jan Chozen. *How to Train a Wild Elephant: And Other Adventures in Mindfulness.* Boston: Shambhala Publications, 2011.

Doolittle, Peter. *How Your "Working Memory" Makes Sense of the World.* TEDGlobal, June 2013. https://www.ted.com/talks/peter_doolittle_how_your_working_memory_makes_sense_of_the_world.

Doyle, Glennon. *Love Warrior.* New York: Flatiron books, 2016.

Gilbert, Elizabeth. *Season 1, Episode 12: Brené Brown on Big Strong Magic.* Magic Lessons Podcast. Posted July 25, 2016. https://www.elizabethgilbert.com/magic-lessons.

Activity 11: Staying Friends with Your Inner Child

Montague, Brad and Robby Novak. *Kid President's Guide to Being Awesome.* New York: HarperCollins, 2015.

Pasricha, Neil. *The Book of Awesome*. New York: Berkley Publishing, 2010.

Rubin, Gretchen. *The Happiness Project: Or, Why I Spent a Year Trying to Sing in the Morning, Clean My Closets, Fight Right, Read Aristotle, and Generally Have More Fun*. New York: HarperCollins, 2009.

Activity 12: The Action Plan

LaPorte, Danielle. *The Fire Starter Sessions: A Soulful and Practical Guide to Creating Success on Your Own Terms*. New York: Harmony Books, 2012.

Sincero, Jen. *You Are a Badass: How to Stop Doubting Your Greatness and Start Living an Awesome Life*. Philadelphia: Running Press, 2013.

ACKNOWLEDGEMENTS

Thank you to my husband, Jason, my son, Nolan, and my second child coming soon, who have all given me the source of joy and encouragement needed to write this book. Thank you to my family, especially my Mom. Thanks for letting me grow up to be a lot like you.

Thank you to the close friends who made me better during my most challenging and invigorating year, Katie and Tegan. You both adopted this introvert, and I thank you for not quitting on me.

Thank you to Dana and Laura, two coaches who helped unravel me and sew me back together. Without you, this awakening may not have happened.

And a big thanks to Morgan Gist MacDonald and the team at Paper Raven Books who helped develop this book to be the best version of itself. Thank you for helping me play bigger.

Made in the USA
San Bernardino, CA
19 October 2018